A Memoir

TRAUMA
IS A
THIEF

A Memoir

TRAUMA
IS A
THIEF

Neal King, PhD

Halo
PUBLISHING
INTERNATIONAL

Halo Publishing International
7550 W IH-10 #800, PMB 2069,
San Antonio, TX 78229

First Edition, September 2024
ISBN: 978-1-63765-644-0
Library of Congress Control Number: 2024914219

The information contained within this book is strictly for informational purposes. Unless otherwise indicated, all the names, characters, businesses, places, events and incidents in this book are either the product of the author's imagination or used in a fictitious manner. Any resemblance to actual persons, living or dead, or actual events is purely coincidental.

Halo Publishing International is a self-publishing company that publishes adult fiction and non-fiction, children's literature, self-help, spiritual, and faith-based books. We continually strive to help authors reach their publishing goals and provide many different services that help them do so. We do not publish books that are deemed to be politically, religiously, or socially disrespectful, or books that are sexually provocative, including erotica. Halo reserves the right to refuse publication of any manuscript if it is deemed not to be in line with our principles. Do you have a book idea you would like us to consider publishing? Please visit www.halopublishing.com for more information.

Dedication

To the memory of my siblings,
Sharon and Ken.

To Peter,
My love, my rock, my best friend.

Contents

Prologue

Trauma is a thief. It robs you — child or adult, no matter your creed, class, gender, or culture of origin, gay or straight — of what might otherwise have been a normal trajectory for your life. It steals your innocence and imparts a deep wound, profoundly affecting your sense of self, from which you will never completely recover.

Trauma can be a single event (mass shooting, rape, car accident) or a series of events over time (experiencing spousal abuse, being held as a hostage, growing up in an abusive family, fighting in a war). Trauma doesn't occur in a vacuum; there will always be a context. Sometimes it's shared — as with the COVID epidemic or in a state of war — when you know that others are experiencing what you are. Other times, you feel as if it's happening to you alone. When it happens within your family, it's the worst — you likely then have no sanctuary to which you can escape and seek protection; it's simply a part of your life.

Whatever its form or context, trauma is invariably a thief. It steals something essential from you that you can never fully recover.

Some will never successfully integrate their trauma into their lives; indeed, trauma takes many lives, both directly and indirectly. Addiction and suicide take the lives of many trauma victims, as do various forms of mental illness. Some victims will spend their lives attempting to flee the effects — or trying to put the pieces back together, with varying degrees of success — unsure exactly what that even means. Trauma can also effectively paralyze you.

It can appear that the trauma survivor has triumphed over whatever happened to them, but actually s/he, in some way, has been driven to create such an appearance — an attempted obfuscation of the ever-deeply felt insult of the trauma — just to function in society. Privately and simultaneously, unseen from the outside, s/he is left with a profound envy of those who have never suffered the same insult. At the same time, paradoxically and simultaneously, some survivors — with work — can genuinely rejoice in and celebrate the good fortune of others.

Trauma often repeats in a vicious cycle, the victim becoming the perpetrator. The complexities of who repeats and who doesn't are myriad.

Persons blessed to live a trauma-free life exist on different planets, in parallel realities, strangers from one another.

If your trauma was in part or in whole sexual, it renders you either hyper- or hyposexual — sends you to one extreme or the other. Intimacy — and the trust that it requires — is compromised and complicated. Sex and intimacy together — in the same place and at the same time — is scary and no small feat.

This book invites you to witness the multiple traumas I suffered and the very troubled family within which I suffered them. I felt entirely alone with my trauma and had no idea that anyone else experienced what I did; it was just my life. I could never imagine anyone helping me.

I invite you to accompany me while my early trauma sends me reeling out into the world, as I try to figure out how to have some sort of normal life — and take back, at least in part, what was stolen from me.

In my case, it's the journey of a middle-class, gay, White, cisgender man who — together with his two siblings — was abruptly abandoned by his mother early in life. Later, my brother and I were sexually abused by our father. I also experienced physical violence at the hands of both my father and brother. Each of us has her/his own particulars.

The other members of my immediate family are all deceased now; each was mortally wounded by our shared trauma — even my father, who was the principal perpetrator. I confess to some survivor guilt.

I have battled mightily to be here today to share this tale with you — in hopes that if you or someone you love has suffered their own trauma, my tale might render some comfort, serve as a resource, or help you feel seen and understood.

Those of us who survive do so differently — in our own way. I became a psychologist and educator and traveled the world — again and again.

While I devised a convincing mask behind which to survive in the world, my inner life was pure tumult for many years. My life out in the world and my life at home were unimaginably different, both as a child and later as a young adult on my own; in both instances, it required me to be an actor and play two very distinct roles.

The gap between those two roles has lessened considerably now, and I have largely shed my mask as I approach eighty — but the new me has been around a lot less time than his actor predecessors.

I share here with you my path toward healing and my strategies for survival — and for remaining as sane and vibrant as one can.

Introduction

Trauma drove both my parents' ancestors — two centuries apart — to leave their homeland and emigrate to the New World. My mother's English ancestors arrived early in the seventeenth century — some of them on the Mayflower. They were escaping the trauma of religious persecution in England. Paradoxically, their countrymen had also visited eight centuries of trauma — in the form of occupation, subjugation, and suppression of the native culture — on Ireland. Way back, my English ancestors include governors of Ireland who oversaw the occupation directly.

My father's Irish ancestors arrived in the late nineteenth century — two and a half centuries after my mother's. They escaped the trauma of famine in Ireland, the effects of which were exacerbated by centuries of harsh English rule.

Once arrived in the New World, the English inflicted enormous trauma on the native peoples of Cape Cod, as they took their lands and replaced the indigenous culture and customs with what they had known in England, essentially replicating what they had done to the Irish. In both instances, the English made themselves at home and — generations later — never questioned their right to their "homeland."

The Irish, already severely traumatized and considered the "unwashed" of Europe, arrived and were shamed and unwelcome — to say the least — in their new land. They left an old trauma behind, only to find a new and oddly familiar one here.

I come from a line of angry Irish men with chips on their shoulders about life not having been fair to them; they were not wrong. Mine was the third generation born in this country. I'll elaborate a bit further on, but this perspective hopefully helps establish the context of my tale.

So trauma is essentially in my DNA. I believe that the trauma I experienced in my family had its roots in prior generations. I struggled for over a decade to find the courage and the right words — and the right voice — to tell this tale.

Demographically, in the mid-1950s, we were a classic post-WWII, newly middle-class, first-house-buying household. I don't recall us ever laughing and having fun as a family. (We did play croquet in the backyard of the house in West LA, but even then, there was little levity.)

Anything remotely cultural was as foreign to us as the moon. There were no plays, concerts, or exhibits — not even movies — that we enjoyed as a family. I never heard anyone in my family sing. In lieu of music, we suffered staticky AM-radio-station fare. When I joined the cast of *Oklahoma* in high school, it was a first — and only — for this family, as far as I know.

TV came of age as we kids did; we progressed from a single square box, where you had to walk across the room to change the channel or adjust the rabbit ears, to far more advanced black-and-white (and eventually color) sets — one in each bedroom, all tuned to different stations — so we didn't even watch TV together.

My mother, from a not-at-all-religious Protestant family, agreed to raise us as Catholics when she married my father. My father went with us to church until I was twelve or so, but after that, we were dropped off and picked up until we could drive — and choose — ourselves.

The Catholic Church — with which I had a love-hate relationship in my early life — introduced me to the world of spirit, which became a vital lifeline for me; I am forever grateful.

We did go to Disneyland in 1956 — the year after it opened — which was a really big deal. Sharon was six, Ken twelve and I nine. On a later visit, I saw Walt Disney showing then-former president Eisenhower around the park, which was also a big deal.

Other than that trip to Disneyland, I don't remember us ever going on a family vacation. We didn't express affection toward one another, verbally or physically. There was a lot of yelling, scolding, and punishment — and a constant accompanying tension, both underlying and on the surface — you just didn't know where, when, or how the next eruption might occur.

I learned to internalize that tension as hypervigilance — constantly on edge/on guard — deep in my body, as a part of my being. This is why so little music lives in my body and why I've always been such a lousy dancer — and have such great admiration for musicians and dancers who seem so exotic to me — and though today I hug and kiss with ease and can also express affection verbally quite naturally, still there is a formality and stiffness to my bearing — by which I hold myself somewhat apart.

As a psychotherapist, I came to call these kinds of effects a somatic reflection of the state of one's psyche — a concept I referenced often with my clients.

Growing up, the only touch I remember in my family was my father's — it was either angry, punishing, hurtful…or hungry, creepy, soul-stealing.

There were no funerals when members of our family died. Our sibling weddings were all small and at home. Sharon attended ours in LA; neither she nor I were aware of or attended Ken's, and neither Ken nor I were aware of or attended hers. They were all very informal affairs.

Though this work is part memoir and part exposé, it isn't intended entirely as either of those. As with any life, mine is filled with interesting stories that could be told here, but to tell the tale at all, I have tried to keep the focus on events, personalities — and their context — that are salient in understanding the disturbed family I survived — and where and how my early years sent me on a bit of a wild ride, flailing out into the world in search of wholeness, identity, intimacy, and safety — together with my lost innocence and youth. My own kind of desultory, Diogenes-like, even alchemical journey.

I have been seeking the archetypal Puer Aeternus my entire life — seeking to somehow reclaim what was stolen from me in my youth. Strong currents of depression, anxiety, and — deepest of them all — shame have been constant companions on this journey. All the while, life had a go at me — testing my mettle, taking my measure.

My tale is offered as a case study — a pulling back of the curtain from the inside — with me as a kind of in-house ethnographer describing what it felt like and how I responded. In the process, I look deeply at the context in which my trauma occurred — within and outside my immediate family. Both a family-systems perspective and an ecological perspective apply.

I write for a few reasons: in the hopes that my words might be helpful to others; for catharsis; because I'm the last surviving member of my family and feel the need to shed light into its darkness; and because I have skills and training that allow the telling of this tale — as researcher, writer, and psychologist — in ways that others might not be able.

I write also to see if I can penetrate the roots of my father's pathologies. He was a career military officer, and while he was a good provider and could be a charming and a good neighbor, he was at the same time truly a monster — a drunk, a bully, and a petty tyrant; a pedophile, and a sociopath — who shamelessly poisoned the lives of his entire family and an unknown number of others.

My mother's stress that led to her role in the family darkness are much more transparent. She was victim and perpetrator. She married the monster, who I believe was smitten with her brother. She did abandon her children and fail to protect them from their father…as she dissolved into drink, depression, and helplessness. She taught me about anhedonia before I knew the word.

I see windows of understanding in the family history across generations, in my father's early life, in his transformation from the wide-eyed young man who wrote to his parents from his cross-country train ride en route to navy boot camp (below) to the hardened adult who was largely incapable of empathy and sought — with insatiable appetite and profound indifference — only to satisfy his own desires.

But did I figure it out and solve the puzzle? I don't think so. Nor did I succeed in my attempts to imagine the internal reality of one who could molest his own children.

So that leaves me to tell the tale and connect the dots as best I can — which I'll try to do with as much candor, compassion, and impartiality as I am able. It's all, of course, through my lens alone; I am an imperfect witness who only knows what I know. I have no doubt that the others would describe their own lives, our life together as a family — and me — in terms different from what you'll encounter here.

Memory too is an imperfect witness — which my psychotherapy clients taught me well. I rely heavily on mine in telling this tale. There's something already deeply amiss in a family that victimizes its own. The sheen of normalcy from the outside serves both to obscure and to compound what's going on inside.

My role in the family was that of the hero — emissary to the outside, star student, articulate and popular guy who had lots of friends — a mask I refined and wore with ease for many years.

Today, happily married and in a relationship since 1997, I am aware of my privilege — my own early trauma notwithstanding. I have written professionally about the intersection of sexual orientation and childhood sexual abuse, and will talk about this topic — including my own struggles with disentangling the two — later in the book.

For now, suffice it to say that there is no evidence that one causes the other. Childhood trauma of any kind will leave permanent scars on its victims, regardless of race, gender, cultural origin, beliefs, or sexual orientation.

I hope this work serves as a testimonial/resource for others who are working to extricate themselves from the detritus of early trauma and trying to put the pieces back together as best they can — and for those who love them and seek to understand their experience.

This has been an uncomfortable book to write, and if I've been successful, it will be an uncomfortable book to read. I have changed the names of a few people to guard their privacy.

And this is only one person's and one family's story — I don't pretend that there's anything generalizable to the experience of other survivors, male or female, and certainly not across cultural nuances — though I do suspect that some will relate to at least parts of what they read herein.

I also feel compelled to acknowledge — here at the get-go — that I have almost certainly, in my own life — albeit unintentionally and likely sometimes without awareness — hurt, disappointed, betrayed the trust of, deepened the confusion of, taken advantage of, caused affront to, led astray…another — for which I am profoundly sorry, and I apologize with all my heart.

My own journey has been driven by the desire to do better, to not visit upon others what has been visited upon me — to not only break the cycle but smash it into smithereens. But I remain a work in progress — even today — and need to express here my heartfelt regret for any and all transgressions along the way.

Because my tale is somewhat chronology and linearity challenged — you might feel, by the end, a bit as if you've been tumbling around in a clothes dryer — but, hey, that's what it's been like.

Please join me as I chart the transformation of a life consumed by trauma's deafening roar into one in which it whispers now instead, ever-present but no longer in control — having long ago made room for universes of love, wonder, appreciation, and beauty of many sorts.

It may seem at times that I've wandered a bit astray — lost my track and direction. My intent here is to provide you with the fullest experience I can conjure of the worlds into which my early life catapulted me, plus detail how I navigated those worlds and how my early life taught me to do so. Any seeming detours are intimately in service to these objectives.

Section One

The Abuse and Its Context

Here we'll spend time in and with my family and experience various sorts and instances of trauma woven inextricably into the fabric of our day-to-day life as a family.

In time, you'll escape the family with me as I stumble along, trying to navigate the larger world, not fully understanding what's happened to me and how it shapes all aspects of my life — knowing all the while that I'm different from others around me.

Each survivor of trauma will have her/his own intimate particulars of their experience; we all share the aftermath in varying degrees.

Part I

In the Beginning

Chapter One
Fire...

Huge flames leapt straight out toward us; it was terrifying and exhilarating.

Sharon was a baby, so Ken had to be six plus and I four or so. The apartment complex in the southern part of La Jolla still stands. Our late father confirmed the incident with a chuckle as we drove past it the last time that he and the three of us were together in San Diego — not long before he died. My late brother likewise confirmed — monosyllabically — that he remembered as well.

In Dad's telling, our mother — then twenty-five or twenty-six — was having an affair and abandoned the three of us. He was overseas with the Navy and had to come back and find her. The fire was evidently in the same complex, in the apartment of a neighbor who took us in.

The fire is my earliest memory. I was standing to my taller older brother's left, paralyzed in awe and terror as flames shot out of the open closet before us. I don't remember before or after, just during. Given our ages at the time, I'm guessing that my brother started it. Per our father, the neighbor turned us over to juvenile authorities, who in turn tracked him down.

My profound shame was born that day. All the world could see that I was unloved, that no one wanted or protected me. I was most of all hurt, heartbroken that I had been cast out, handed over to strangers, removed from my home.

I of course had no idea where our parents were; I just knew that they had abandoned us — and something vital closed in my little-boy heart. From that day forward, the stage was set: they could not be trusted — and I wasn't sure that anyone else could be either. I was on my own and had to navigate the world by myself.

My parents both eventually reappeared physically. As far as I was concerned, they were physical presences only; all bonds of attachment had been severely compromised.

These events — and their precursors — became the foundation for our life as a family…and for my own life as I became an essentially solitary person, even in a crowd or amongst friends, even — in moments — in my most intimate relationships.

My aunt Jeanne — widow of my mother's older brother, born in late 1925, and the last surviving member of my parents' generation in our family — told me that both my mother and older brother had come — once separately, once together — to stay for varying lengths of time with Mom's parents in Clinton, Massachusetts, during some periods of unspecified strain in our parents' marriage.

I learned in my training as a psychologist that fire setting is a classic behavior of a child who has been abandoned. Ken, my older brother, was angry and detached all of his life that I knew him. Per our father, he had been a happy only child who turned very unhappy when I arrived. He was always jealous of me, partly because I was more socially fluent and

popular with my peers. There were times that he was physically violent with me.

...And Its Aftermath...

A young child who is abandoned by her/his parents is terrified and bewildered; at our ages, there was no capacity to
understand what happened. We would have felt that it was
our fault, that we caused it. These feelings became the core of
our identities. Ken, who was the oldest, might also have felt
angry — again — with enough sense of pre-abandonment
reality to understand that something vital had been taken
from him.

For me, these very feelings dwell today — uninterrupted
— in the depths of my being and sense of self — often well
hidden, sometimes making a sudden surprise appearance —
to my own bewilderment and that of those who happen
to witness that particular moment. It's as if that little boy
momentarily surfaces, rips off my mask, and takes control.
I become sad and deflated.

For my poor brother, I understand now that he must have
felt abandoned by my birth, by our collective abandonment
at the time of the fire, by being left with our grandparents —
all compounded by his molestation as a boy by our father,
who was his role model and something of a hero to him. He
disliked and was disdainful of our mother — to the point of
verbal and even physical abuse when an adolescent — perhaps also not surprisingly. So, essentially, he had only one

"real" parent to whom he clung — who was also his abuser — as he experienced the world.

I saw in my late sister's struggle with alcoholism in her sixties — the same scourge that hastened our mother's death and killed our father and older brother — the residue of this early experience as — in the depths of her depression, as in her worst binges — she felt worthless, dejected, ashamed, and alone. Hers was a classic Eros-Thanatos battle; with much chemo, radiation, and surgery, she survived two bouts of breast cancer and one of non-Hodgkin's lymphoma, plus a terminal and slowly metastasizing cancer in her depleted and daily under-attack liver.

She and I had been very close throughout our lives — she was my one friend in the family; I was also her big-brother protector. I felt that her various illnesses stole her from me, and, now that she's gone, feel abandoned and cheated that she is no longer here.

Her late father-in-law once commented that he would have traded all three of his sons for her as a daughter. Most of her life, she was the most gentle, considerate, generous, fun-loving, unselfish, and caring person you could imagine. Her laugh was hearty and contagious.

Our father was a sexist racist, a fairly typical product of his generation and working-class, immigrant family background. He made fun of Sharon's breasts when they started to develop and didn't think that girls needed to go to college since they were just going to get married and have children. Sharon was very talented artistically; I lobbied for art school for her — to no avail.

Our mother was from a similar blue-collar background as Dad; she got along when young with neither her mother nor her older brother, though she loved and idolized her father. She was depressed and drank heavily much of our childhood — so wasn't particularly credible or attractive as a role model, or as a parent for that matter.

In his pedophilia, Dad clearly preferred boys, ideally in the six-to-twelve range, so I doubt that Sharon was molested by him, as her brothers were. She had no memory of any molestation. He was her preferred parent, and they seemed to enjoy a pretty easy and comfortable relationship most of their lives. Both my brother and sister shared our father's handy and technical talents and inclinations, whereas my father's description of my "not knowing which end of a screwdriver to hold on to" was only a mild exaggeration.

For myself, I had good reason to trust neither parent — even though I was my mother's favorite and was very fond of her and her good heart in spite of her less attractive qualities.

Once, in grammar school, we were having some sort of physical examination, so a group of us boys were standing around in our underwear behind a screen erected in a classroom or hallway in the school. Somehow, the screen fell or was knocked over, and there we all were, exposed to the passersby. I was mortified with shame, embarrassment, and powerlessness to escape the situation. I can't say for sure what the others experienced, but am pretty sure today that I experienced this episode as containing many of the same elements of what followed the fire much earlier in life. Ignominy was reinforced exponentially in my inner life.

I had a breakthrough of sorts, at seventy, in realizing that my own depression also contains these same elements:

feeling abandoned, alone, unloved, trapped, ashamed, pow-erless — all, I firmly believed in my darkest moments, fully visible from the outside to others, like my siblings. I had never seen this so clearly before. Of course, we three siblings are/were all very different, and there is a multiplicity of fac-tors that defined and shaped each of our lives, but I believe today that our common foundation/origins are more than purely genetic. A new empathy for my brother has been born from this breakthrough.

In terms of our mother, I think of Jung's observation that "nothing has a stronger influence psychologically on their environment and especially on their children than the unlived life of the parent." In other words, most parents are themselves children raising children. Mom was married at eighteen, had her first child at nineteen, her second a month before turning twenty-two, and all three by twenty-five.

While my brother and I were clearly the product of our parents, my sister — blonde and blue-eyed as she was — and I wondered if she might have had a different father. We talked about getting her DNA tested, but never actually did.

Work was my addiction — and I credit my boundless curi-osity, love of travel, learning in general, people, the arts, etc., with my relative sanity and mental health. I was once given the nickname NNN, Nearly Normal Neal. I feel very fortunate.

I credit my training as a psychologist, together with my explorations in and practice of mindfulness meditation, with my having been able to get inside and underneath of a life-long, debilitating, and recurring depression of this depth and early etiology. It's exactly what I would seek to do with clients during my years of practice as a psychotherapist, with varying degrees of success. In my opinion, one never escapes or fully extricates oneself from early trauma, but one can diminish the hold of the darkness — considerably — by applying the skills and understanding as an adult that none of us has as small children.

The earlier the origins — particularly when we're talking preverbal and primitive stages of cognitive ability (which would have been my sister's experience) — the more difficult the task. My breakthrough having come at age seventy, after years of study and multiple sorts of therapies, testifies to the density of the defenses that necessarily build around such early insult and their pugnacity in keeping us from the insult itself — except while experiencing the murk of depression. The ancient fear of being engulfed by our trauma necessitates a stalwart defensive structure, even as adults.

As I would say to clients, as adults, we have so much more in terms of resources to combat early trauma than we did as the children whose direct experience required us to shield and protect ourselves. In my case, each day reveals how what I understand today, but did not yesterday, affects — and improves — my experience of myself in the day-to-day.

Chapter Two
Uncle Mac

My Uncle Mac (Gordon Clifford) would have turned one hundred in December 2023. He graduated from Clinton (Massachusetts) High School in 1941, with the nickname Patch, at age seventeen — a year before his younger sister, Ellen, my mother, who was also seventeen when she graduated with the nickname Tootie.

Per Mac, the two siblings were not close and "ran with different crowds." Their respective high school yearbooks describe Mac as "happy-go-lucky…debonair…not an athlete" and as having the high ambition to serve in the navy as a "skilled technician"; and Ellen as "one of the most attractive girls of the senior class" whose "favorite pastime" is roller skating, and who "plans to enter Becker College in the fall."

Neither of their parents graduated from high school. Mac joined the US Navy, as his father had done before him — I'm guessing pretty much right out of high school. He was a boyishly handsome, upbeat young man. In the navy, he met my father, Roy, who had also enlisted after high school and was nearly five years Mac's senior. He was also a charming and handsome young man who hailed, coincidentally, from a different Clinton — in Iowa.

The two sailors became friends. Mac at some point invited my father home with him when both were on leave. Roy and Ellen were wed in June 1943, with Mac and his then soon-to-be first wife, Barbara, as their best man and maid of honor. At the time of the wedding, Ellen was eighteen, Mac nineteen, and Roy twenty-four.

Mac died in 2012 at the age of eighty-eight, Roy in 1990 at age seventy-one, and Ellen in 1978 at age fifty-three. Mac died from natural causes, Roy from an esophageal hemorrhage due to his acute alcoholism, and Ellen from multiple cancers, cirrhosis of the liver, and acute alcoholism.

Mac and Barbara had a daughter, Maureen, who died from alcoholism in 2009 at age sixty-five, leaving an estranged adopted daughter. Mac and his second wife, Jeanne, wed in 1949 and had no children. After living during their working lives in an apartment above his parents' home in Clinton, they retired to West Yarmouth, Massachusetts, and a charming Cape Cod bungalow they had purchased while both were still working. They had both fallen in love with Cape Cod during visits there with Jeanne's older brother, Raymond, and his family. Mac spent most of his retirement on the Cape as a nearly full-time volunteer at the local hospital; he was a much-loved part of the community.

I'll go into more depth and detail about these folks' lives and deaths further on, but wanted to preview here what I lived amidst, in aggregate. I'm the middle child and your narrator.

Roy, my father, spent his seventieth birthday in county jail in Central California for his attempted molestation of two neighborhood boys, both around ten years of age. He had earlier molested both of his sons — as well as at least one other neighborhood boy — over a period of several years. He was known by the family to be suspiciously solicitous of young male nephews and great-nephews on his periodic visits to his hometown of Clinton, Iowa.

Jeanne, Uncle Mac's second wife, was born in late 1925 and, at this writing, is in assisted living at Decatur House in Sandwich, Massachusetts — where she is the oldest resident and the one with longest tenure in the house. She has macular degeneration and walks with a cane, but is sharp as a tack, loves to laugh, and is always up for an outing with visiting family members. She is — and has always been — an absolute love. Sandwich is the oldest town on Cape Cod. I go to visit her at least every other year, and we speak often on the phone, always on Sunday mornings — when she has the fewest number of her daytime TV programs to keep her busy.

Jeanne's older brother, Raymond, and sister, Christine, left five and four children, respectively, making Jeanne — as the last of her generation — the much beloved yet unwitting matriarch of the clan, which today includes your humble scribe, Jeanne's nine blood nieces and nephews, and numerous great-nephews and -nieces as well as, recently, her first great-great-niece.

So Mac and the US Navy wound up bringing his sister's family into existence and, today, its one survivor into Jeanne's loving family — albeit by marriage and somewhat as the mutt of the clan.

Mac and Ellen were born in Harrisville, New Hampshire — Mac in his parents' small apartment in the center of town and Ellen fourteen months later in her maternal grandparents' home on Peanut Row, five homes across from Harrisville

Pond and just down the road from Sunset Beach. Peanut Row was owned by their grandparents' and parents' common employer: Cheshire (textile) Mill, owned and operated by the Colony family. Their father, Wilmot Clifford, classic Swamp Yankee that he was, had migrated south from his native Maine in search of work. Their mother, Florence, left high school to work in the mill's employee boarding house and help support her family — where she met her future husband, Wilmot.

Wilmot wasn't content to stay and raise his family in Harrisville, however — for whatever reason, not caring for the mill — so the southward migration continued. Wilmot and Florence raised their two children in Clinton, Massachusetts, where Wilmot worked at a series of factory jobs. His retirement notice indicates that "Macklin started his Palmer Plant service in 1925 as a tinner. He was made foreman of the Venetian Blind Department in 1938, foreman of the Coburn Department in 1946, and foreman of the Coburn and Vibrating departments in 1961." Wilmot died in Clinton in 1974, at age seventy-three, of emphysema.

Florence's parents stayed in their Peanut Row house — where into his high school years, Mac would often spend summers with them — until their own deaths. They — Harry Sturtevant and Ann (Sharp) Sturtevant — are buried in nearby Keene, New Hampshire, close to their son, Harry, and his wife, Mafalda. Harry was a well-known local character, driving his almost always new or nearly new convertible around town. He was eighty-nine when he died in 1971, having survived his beloved wife, Annie, by over twenty years.

Mac gave me — on one visit with him and Jeanne at their home on the Cape — a manila folder with a couple of sheets of paper with handwritten notes laying out what he knew of their family history. Detailed thereon were the prior two generations…period.

On another of my many visits with Mac and Jeanne on the Cape, Mac asked me to take a ride with him — during which he confided to me, with obvious discomfort, that my father had been one of a group of men investigated by the navy for allegations of homosexual behavior. It was my impression at the time that Mac had not been amongst those investigated — and that no serious adverse conclusions had been reached, as Roy retired from the navy in 1959, after twenty-two years of service. Nonetheless, this secret seemed to have weighed heavily on Mac for years, and he needed for me to know. My father had died by this time.

During my undergraduate years in the SF Bay Area, Mac and Jeanne would stop over when on a cruise or changing flights for Hawaii or some other westward destination, and the three of us would always enjoy a lively night out — a joyous tradition that continued into later life. On one of these later visits, I told Mac and Jeanne about Roy's arrest for attempted child molestation, which led to his incarceration at the time of his seventieth birthday. It is my recollection that Jeanne was stunned and Mac simply silent. More on these events, in context, a bit further along.

Curious to learn more about the King and Macklin family lineage, I delved — aided by my academic training as a researcher, the wonders of the Internet, and DNA-enabled searching — deeply into a genealogical quest — which took me places and across centuries that I could not have anticipated at the outset, and worlds beyond the contents of the manila folder that Mac handed me that day at their home in West Yarmouth. I had not even that much information on the King side.

There are ironies in what I learned on the Macklin side — ones that I have been able to share with Jeanne, but wish I could have shared with Mac and Ellen when they were alive.

Florence's lineage is all England — despite her father's Dutch name. The Sturtevant family's English origins can be traced to fifteenth-century North Central England; they arrived in North America in the seventeenth century, not long after the *Mayflower* landed on Cape Cod. They married into some of the families descendant from *Mayflower* passengers (Standish, Warren, Winslow) and spent generations in and around Plymouth, Massachusetts — just across the Sagamore Bridge from where Mac is interred (and Jeanne will join him) at Massachusetts National Cemetery in Bourne. There is a Sturtevant Cemetery in Halifax, just west of Plymouth — dating from 1728 — where surely early settler relations are buried. Much less is known about Florence's mother's Sharp line, except that they originated in the Leeds and Kent areas of England.

Wilmot's family name, Macklin, is an offshoot of the MacLean clan, Isle of Mull, Scotland. Like many Scots who migrated to North America, the Macklins arrived in New Brunswick, Canada, in the early eighteenth century. Wilmot's father, Ora (born in Maine, died in Massachusetts), married Ellen Grace Brown, who died at age twenty-seven, having by then given birth to Wilmot as well as his older brother and younger sister. Ellen Grace (my mother was Ellen Ann, named after her two grandmothers) was descendant from *Mayflower* passengers John Howland and Elizabeth Tilley, whose daughter, Hope, married John Hale Chipman. John Howland is buried in Plymouth; his wife, Elizabeth, in East Providence, Rhode Island; and (Elder) John Chipman at the old cemetery in Sandwich — where Jeanne has been in residence at Decatur House. So Mac, unbeknownst to him, shared and shares his beloved Cape Cod with generations of ancestors.

Research into Ellen Grace Brown's lineage gave the most robust results of all my grandparents' lines; its multiple tributaries can be traced throughout much of England, back to the thirteenth and fourteenth centuries, and include generations in London proper, as well as royal households and — ironically, given the King family roots — governors of Ireland, as I mentioned earlier. Generations of my immediate family were entirely unaware of these details.

In retrospect, early visits to the Cape when Mac was still alive fell innocently into the ignorance-is-bliss category in that they were overwhelmingly about visiting family — Florence lived there with Mac and Jeanne until her death at eighty-nine, in 1995, from old age complicated by dementia — with a couple of trips to Provincetown just for fun. I always found the Cape some combination of enchanting and exotic, likely fueled in part by having grown up with the glamorous mystique of the Kennedy family and their compound in Hyannis.

On one recent visit — in May 2023 — to visit Jeanne in Sandwich, I stopped at the Sturtevant Cemetery in Halifax on the drive down from Boston. I was aware of the significance of Chipman Lane off Route 6A and visited the Old

Cemetery in Sandwich, knowing that Elder John Chipman, my ninth-great-grandfather, was buried there.

I'd also learned about the Nauset and Wampanoag peoples who had made the Cape their home for thousands of years before the English settlers arrived in the seventeenth century, destroying their culture and way of life — and replacing them with their own.

On the same visit, I stood atop a tall sand dune mid-beach in East Sandwich, on a clear and blustery day, where one could look left and right over Cape Cod Bay and imagine both the arrival there of the *Mayflower*'s surviving passengers in November of 1620 — as they attempted to figure out where best to land and go ashore — and the heretofore undisturbed lives of the Cape's indigenous peoples, destined by this ship's arrival — and the many that followed — for tragic oblivion.

The Cape has become for me less innocent and far more complex. I do take comfort from the fact that Mac's eternal resting place is there, with his/our ancestors, by far, the most recent arrivals in the lineage.

Roy's lineage stands in sharp contrast to Ellen's. Though both were working-class and therefore not highly educated, Roy's ancestors arrived as immigrants escaping poverty, lack of opportunity, and the unrelenting cruelties of their occupiers — all in the mid to late nineteenth century. Ellen's, originally escaping religious persecution in England, had by then spawned generations over the two-plus centuries since their arrival in North America — and considered themselves right at home.

By the time the couple met, Ellen's was a comfortably confident and well-established line — blissfully oblivious to its origins — with all that that implies — while Roy's was still struggling for acceptance and survival, trying to find its bearings and its way — all too mindful of its still-recent impoverished roots, residual shame, and struggles not too far beneath the surface.

Roy and his younger brother, John, were angry men; reportedly, both their father, John, and grandfather John were as well. Roy went through life with a distinctive chip on his shoulder, always seeming to feel that he was being slighted, wronged, and cheated.

Though not obvious — or perhaps even conscious — these ancestral factors had to have played a role in the psychological makeup of the two people who became my parents — and had to have been a factor in their relationship.

I suppose it's accurate to say that neither line was exactly welcome from the perspective of those who were here before them, and equally safe to say that Ellen's ancestors arrived as conquerors of the indigenous peoples of Eastern Massachusetts; they, in turn, having conquered and taken the new land as their own, did not exactly receive the later-arriving Irish — whose lands they had occupied for eight centuries — with open arms.

The Irish ancestors started at the bottom of the ladder and, rung by rung, struggled to assimilate and earn acceptance by their fellow Europeans (by whom they were considered inferior, even in Europe) who by then had staked their claim to the country.

It's of course a huge leap from the ancient and hallowed kings of the west of Ireland, the ancestral line of legend of the

King family, to their descendant railway granger from land-locked County Roscommon — my great-great-grandfather King — whose eldest son would emigrate to the USA by sea in the late nineteenth century, his family impoverished by the centuries-old English occupation and a devastating nineteenth-century famine, both of which ravished the country.

It's another leap, albeit one of far fewer generations, from that first-of-his-line, new immigrant to his grandson, my father, who plays so large a role in this narrative.

I sketch the ancestral background here in hopes of providing context and possibly contributing factors to help explain who my father was and why he lived the life he did.

Chapter Three
Go West, Young Man

Los Angeles Limited, en route through Nevada,
Mar 14, 1937

Dear Mom and Dad,

Here's another, we're on the UPRR now and just going through the Rockies.

Had a swell trip since I left Des Moines. We had a layover in Denver and Salt Lake City, each of a couple of hours and we went through the Rockies last night and so far, we have gone through twenty-eight tunnels on one railroad [sic] one was more than six miles long, and 5,000 feet above sea level and 4,000 feet under the top of the mountain.

After we got out of the tunnel, we stopped in a mountain town and got out for a short stroll.

We will arrive in LA about 8:30 in the AM and take another train for San Diego, in which we will arrive at a little after 12.

I tried to get to go to mass today in Salt Lake, I had the time but there wasn't a church within close enough distance that had mass at the right time so I couldn't go.

We have been traveling across a desert all day without a tree in sight just sage brush and mountains in the background.

Well, sometime tomorrow I should have my address and Company number and when I do, I'll write again and let you know.

Tell John, Gene and Bernard and the kids hello.

Bye and Love, Roy

Two months after his eighteenth birthday, and nine months after his high school graduation, Roy is headed across the country by train to begin navy boot camp in San Diego — never to return to Clinton (unlike two of his brothers), except for occasional visits.

Someone somewhere told me/us that Roy had missed appointment to the US Naval Academy by "one-quarter of a point." I'm honestly to this day not sure what that means, but he was supposedly embittered by this near miss the rest of his life.

But in his young missive above, one senses neither bitterness nor the darkness that characterized much of Roy's adult life. Instead, there is the sense of a dutiful and wide-eyed young man off on a grand adventure. Six years would elapse before he wed Ellen, with young Mac at his side.

As Roy wrote this letter, he had five living siblings: Bernard and Gene were his older brothers, John and George his younger brothers, and La Rayne his younger and only sister. La Rayne and George were "the kids" referred to in his letter.

Gene, the second oldest, driving a car whose ownership he shared with Bernard, would die at age twenty in an early morning, single-car accident three months after Roy's letter was written; La Rayne, the second youngest, died from leukemia six years after, at age twenty-one, just months after Roy and Ellen were married.

Years later, I asked Roy if he had returned to Clinton for his brother Gene's funeral (not realizing that he would have just begun his military service at the time), and he responded somewhat angrily, "No, why would I?" I remain today uncertain what history and emotion was behind this reaction, though later had the impression that he had been jealous of Gene.

Bernard and John returned to Clinton after their time in the navy and married sisters Dorothy and Pearl Jackson; they both raised their families there. Bernard and Dorothy had two sons, Terry and James, and one daughter, Renee. John and Pearl had two sons, John and Robert, and two daughters, Jeanne and Theresa.

I have knowledge at this writing of male childhood sexual abuse having afflicted three of the brothers' families, within the family, in my generation — which leads me to suspect strongly that there is a much larger story to be told than I have the information to tell here. My father, as far as I know, was the only brother to have perpetrated sexual abuse.

The Clinton cousins raved about the fun times they enjoyed together with the large and boisterous Jackson clan, and how they hated being told they had to go visit the King grandparents because they would "just sit there" when they did. We, from our California perspective, were oblivious to this dynamic.

George married local girl Lorraine Scholtes; their two children, Maureen and Murray, were born in Clinton — before the family moved to California, where both children graduated high school and live today with their families.

Roy married the only out-of-town girl and was the only one whose children were all born elsewhere (Ken in Georgia, Neal in Florida, and Sharon in California — all places where Roy was stationed at the time).

Roy was the first and youngest of the four surviving brothers to die, at seventy-one. Ellen, at fifty-three, was the first and youngest of the wives to die. Ken, at forty-seven, was the first and youngest of the King cousins to die and Sharon the second, at age sixty-six.

Bernard was ninety-two, John seventy-six, and George eighty-five when they died. With one unknown — John's younger daughter, Theresa, who is the second-youngest cousin and estranged from her family — all of the other cousins are alive and well at this writing — with Terry, the oldest, born in 1940, and Robert, the youngest, in 1960. Terry and Jeanne still live in Clinton; James and Renee nearby.

Roy's parents, John and Mary, were twenty and nineteen, respectively, when they were married in Clinton; John died at age ninety in 1985 — and Mary at age ninety-four in 1990. Mary was a devout Catholic and very active in her parish activities throughout her life.

Mary's maiden name was Simmert — her mother was born Mary Emma Croughan, the family from the Galway area of Western Ireland. We always assumed that Mary was half Irish and half German, BUT my DNA testing came back showing NO German at all.

Mary's birth occurred within months of her parents' wedding. Her mother was previously married to William Clark, with whom she had a son, also William, born four years before Mary. The senior Clark was of Scottish-Irish-English descent and lived in Clinton until Mary was nearly forty. I suspect that he was Mary's father. We'll never know for sure, and who knew what even then remains a mystery.

As noted, John's father, also John, the eldest of seven known siblings, emigrated from County Roscommon, Ireland, at age twenty in 1883.

My grandfather John Joseph worked as a machinist for the East Iowa Division of the Chicago Northwestern Railroad Line that passed through Clinton. John Joseph's father, John, reportedly also worked for the railroad in Clinton, as his own father had done in Ireland.

My great-grandfather John initially joined one of his mother's brothers and his wife, John and Mary Fulton (believed to be the first of our relations to come to the USA), outside of Peoria, Illinois, before settling in the Clinton area. He married an Irish widow in Clinton, Anna Gardner, whose family hailed from County Mayo, adjacent to County Roscommon.

The 1901 Census of Ireland shows his parents, "Michael (62) and Ellen (60)," and his siblings "Mary (34), Michael (30), and James (21)" still in their household in the townland of Rusheen, near Boyle, eighteen years after John departed. Michael Sr.'s occupation was listed as "railway granger," Michael Jr.'s as "railway miles man," and James's as "farmer."

John Sr.'s younger brother, Patrick — the only other of the siblings reported to have crossed the Atlantic — is shown as having died in Providence, Rhode Island, at age eighteen or nineteen in 1887. Unfortunately, nothing more is known about this young man — including whether he crossed the ocean with his older brother in 1883.

Michael King (1908–1988), my grandfather's first cousin, son of his uncle Michael — is the last known of our direct line to have lived and died in Ireland. I first visited Ireland in 1974, but knew next to nothing about the family history. I have regretted ever since that, had I been better informed at the time, I could certainly have met this last Michael King.

I did however have the opportunity, on a return visit to Ireland in 2002 (my third), to meet with folks who remembered the last of our Kings — including Michael (and his father and grandfather, both Michaels) — who was found dead on a street in Galway at age eighty, evidently having been drinking heavily and then robbed.

Never married, this Michael was a traveling salesman who, after WWII, had a one-room office in Dublin and acted as an agent for various firms, including (from a letter sent by a surviving, much younger friend) "Garrets Tea; Stafford

Salt, Spice and Cereals; and Jackson's Bar Fittings." He traveled the west, northwest, Midland, and east regions of Ireland during this time.

He inherited — and subsequently sold to a Patrick Kelly — the King residence in Rusheen and the small plot on which it sat.

A staff member at the National Archives in Dublin remarked, upon handing me some requested information about the King land in Rusheen, "No wonder they left — they had almost nothing there." The English had taken possession of most of the land that belonged to the Irish, eventually adopting the Quarter-Acre Clause — working Irish could own no more than that if they wished to receive assistance under the Poor Law Amendment Act during the Great Irish Famine.

On one of my visits to Ireland, local friends showed me a Mass rock — used by priests as an altar upon which to clandestinely say Mass, a practice forbidden by the English — stark and further evidence of Irish privation under their English overlords.

The King property subsequently changed hands a number of times, and is owned and occupied today — to the horror of our friends in Rusheen — by an English family!

In Boyle, Michael also at one time owned a pub — since converted into a convenience store — in which he worked as a youth. He, like his parents, is buried in an unmarked grave in Eastersnow Cemetery, between Rusheen and Croghan, together with prior generations of Kings, whose own gravestones have been swallowed up by the peat soil there.

I still hope to one day order and have installed a gravestone for Michael, with an inscription that would read:

Michael King
1908–1988
King of the Road and Last of the Line

At the time of my great-grandfather John and Anna's marriage, in 1892, Anna had lost three children and her first husband, Frank Murray. Later, she and John lost three infants and saw four other children grow into adulthood — James Bernard, John Joseph (my grandfather), Mary Ellen, and Michael Peter.

Roy's Early Life

As with my mother, I have relatively few anecdotes about my father's early life. He was almost eleven years old when the financial markets crashed in October 1929. We heard stories as kids of his having to shamefully scrounge along the railroad tracks for bits of coal to help keep the family warm, and of there often being not enough for the family to eat.

He kept, as an adult — and glowed when showing it to me — a crude wood carving of the Boy Scout emblem, which had been painted gold against the wood base from which it had been carved. Did he do the carving? Was it a gift? Why did this piece of his childhood remain precious to him so many years later?

I have his yearbooks (they were amongst his papers, so he kept them) from his junior and senior years at Saint Mary's High School, in Clinton, Iowa. He graduated with the class of 1936, so would have been seventeen at the time. Both books are signed by lots of classmates and several nuns. His senior book is also signed by one of the three priests pictured, the Reverend Raymond Murphy, a young priest — then in his second year in Clinton — who evidently worked with the local Boy Scout troops.

There were twenty-seven pictured in his junior-class photo from 1935, eleven girls and sixteen boys. Roy is dressed smartly in suit and tie, like the other boys, his dark, wavy hair combed back from his forehead. Opposite the page with the basketball and football teams, he stands (in sharp contrast) in his Scout uniform, in the back row of the Troop 111 photo.

In his senior yearbook, next to his very handsome graduation photo, is this list of his school activities: "Junior Holy Name Society, '33–'36; Blugold Staff — Business Manager, Ad Solicitor, '36; Vergil Club, '35; Delegate to the Catholic Students Mission Crusade Convention, '35." Underneath this list is this quotation: "Art is long and time is fleeting." His signature, "Roy King '36" is written over the text.

There are eleven boys and nine girls pictured as the class of 1936. There is a photo captioned "Boy Scout Troops," which does not include him.

The class prophecy includes this mention: "Again I return you to Tin Pan Alley, New York City, where we shall visit the studio of the famous artist, LeRoy King. The picture he is seen working on is for the Chicago Art Institute." I never knew him as particularly creative or at all interested in the arts; he was very skilled in more technical ways.

The class will includes this bequest: "I, Leroy King, leave my position as draftsman to Arthur Ries" (a junior pictured in the Boy Scout Troop 108 photo in Roy's junior yearbook).

Roy attended his fiftieth high school class reunion, in Clinton, in May of 1986. His father had died the prior year; his mother would have still been alive. My mother had died nearly eight years before. The reunion program lists seventeen surviving class members and six deceased; twelve attended the reunion. Roy noted that nine girls and eight boys left Clinton; he also taped two photos from the event into his yearbook, including the group photo with him standing somewhat sheepishly third from the right, back row.

As mentioned, John Sr., John Joseph, Roy, and his brother John Raymond were all known as angry men — each was referred to as "one of the angry King men." I witnessed an exchange between Roy and his father that illustrated this dynamic. Sharon; her then toddler daughter, Leia; Roy; and I were visiting Clinton to celebrate Roy's mother's ninetieth birthday in 1985. We were staying at a local hotel, but one evening, having enjoyed an early dinner with Bernard and Dorothy, we stopped back at Roy's parents' house. As soon as we walked through the door, Roy's father (aged ninety, only ten weeks before his death) flew into a rage, wanting to know where we'd been so late and berating Roy that his mother had been "worried sick." Roy, then sixty-six, flew immediately into a corresponding rage, stating how early it still was and declaring no obligation to check in with them. I stepped between the two men and pushed Roy toward the kitchen, saying, "Go talk with your mother." It was clear to me that we had just witnessed an old pattern wherein each triggered the other.

His entire life, as an angry man, Roy was easily enraged. His brothers Bernard and George were easygoing, as were his uncle Michael (who ran a local pub in Clinton) and aunt Marie, who was an absolute love.

Roy and John were the two alcoholics in the family and the two middle children. Roy kept — in addition to the

1937 letter to his parents and a very poignant letter from his sister La Rayne, dated February 1943 (seven months before her death) — an undated and very big-brother letter that I believe was written to his younger brother, John, regaling him with tales from his adventures with the navy on a South America cruise.

James Joyce called the Irish "a priest-ridden race," and the world has seen the horrific abuse inflicted upon Irish children — particularly those in the church's care, most especially in boarding schools, across generations, by their priests. We'll never know if Roy's young priest in Clinton abused him, or if his grandfather brought with him across the sea some memory or scars from his own childhood in Ireland.

Chapter Four
We Moved A Lot

"We Moved A Lot" is the title of my chapter in my poet friend Franklin Abbott's early '90s anthology, *Boyhood: Growing Up Male, A Multicultural Anthology*. He asked his contributors to reflect on some particularly salient cultural aspect of their boyhood. His editors initially balked at my chapter's being sufficiently "cultural" — until we pointed out that this was an aspect of military culture, and the culture of military families.

Below are excerpts from that chapter, offering a now thirty-plus-year-old perspective on our physical moves as a young family — under the command of my father — and some of the darker undercurrents as they developed and manifested in our shared life. My father, brother, and sister were all still alive when this was written.

> *There are several places I do remember. Three in Connecticut stand out at the moment. One approaches the magical in my memory; it was rural, nearest to a town I remember being named Ledyard. Our nearest neighbors were farmers, some distance down the road. I had a playmate there; we disturbed a*

bee or hornets' nest one day and I remember being very frightened. There were woods which seemed to go on forever behind our house; I was free to imagine them haunted or enchanted or inviting or forbidding, depending upon my own state and need. I don't remember being old enough to freely explore them. I was old enough to take a pail across the road and pick berries, I guess with my parents and older brother. Were they blueberries or raspberries? They were delicious to eat while picking, turned hands and mouths delightfully amusing colors, and got cooked into pies and desserts. Those berries were great fun; the place and the time I remember as innocent, full of wonder, safe. I think we didn't stay there long, though I don't know why. It seemed pretty normal to pick up and move when I was a child, so I doubt I questioned it. I think New London was next, or maybe it was La Jolla and the birth of my sister and then back to Connecticut.

I remember my sister being in both New London and Groton, and don't remember her at all in Ledyard, so maybe La Jolla was next. There, I remember an older woman who stayed with us a lot; she and I helped my sister take her first steps. I also remember setting fire to a neighbor's clothes closet, with my older brother. Recently, my father, brother and I were in San Diego to celebrate my sister's 40th birthday. With her, we drove past the La Jolla apartments where we lived when she was born and when we set the fire. My father, seeming to find humor in the recollection, asked if we remembered. My sister didn't; my brother and I did. My own reconstruction from memory and anecdotes is that we had been left with these neighbors shortly after my sister's birth. My father was out of the country; my mother evidently simply didn't come back for us. According to my father, the neighbors eventually turned us over to juvenile authorities; he also says he was called back to the States to find our mother, and eventually did, in a bar. According to him, she'd been having an affair. I recall this as a mixed time, bright with the arrival of my sister, dark with abandonment and fear.

New London, then, had a shakier foundation than the brief time in Ledyard; I guess there were no other innocent periods, let alone safe. My folks had rented a large house near the beach, in the winter. Several rooms were closed off and I resented it, feeling shut out. I wondered what was in those rooms, and felt that we were somehow lacking, not to be able to have the whole house. I learned to roller skate in New London; my closest friends were two Jewish girls, sisters. We skated together, I with a pillow fastened to my butt, an obvious commentary on my beginning skating skills. My brother was in school; my sister and I weren't. He was exposed to Scarlet Fever, but didn't contract it. My sister and I did. I remember a sun porch (on the third floor?) where we convalesced; this became a pattern, as much by natural inclination as circumstance: my sister and I together, sharing experience; our brother apart. Grandparents came to the New London house and I remember a Christmas which feels warm and happy. I see a fire (in the fireplace) and the glow feels warm, the people in the recollection feel relaxed. I don't remember other Christmases feeling like that. The Atlantic Ocean was across and down the street; I loved, in winter, standing against the seawall and feeling mesmerized by the dark green waters and their sometimes soft sometimes furious waves; I loved the salt in the wind, the way it stayed in my hair and on my lips after I was back snugly in the house. The Pacific Ocean is more blue, but I suffer the same paralysis today, gladly, as I stand and let it take me outside of myself, as the Atlantic did then. I remember too an amusement park down the street, but I think it was closed, because of the season; it feels like the rooms in the house, something there but not there, a tease, something I didn't get to have.

Groton was less dramatic. My brother broke his leg one day as we both were riding our bikes to school. I raced home on mine only to find that someone had called after he fell and my mother was on her way to him. He recuperated on the front porch, and my sister and I had bunk beds in our shared bedroom. Once, from the top bunk, I leaned outside the open doorway and looked into the living room where my parents sat (talking? kissing!!?? watching television?). My mother screamed at me to get back to bed with a tone which sent cold terror into my heart. It cemented a knowing I had already, from La Jolla, that she wasn't safe; I couldn't trust her, and had to keep some part of me free and protected from her. I remember school being closed due to snow, and sledding on the hills near the house. The neighbors had a boxer named "Stormy," and we turned our needs to love and hold onto him. I remember "Stormy" spending lots of time in the Groton house, and was happy he was there. From the classroom window I remember one day being able to watch the launching of the (nuclear?) submarine "Nautilus." I think Maime Eisenhower broke a bottle of Champagne over the bow. The adults were very excited about this event; I think the teacher said something about us witnessing history. I remember thinking it was odd to break a tiny bottle on a big ship; I wondered if everybody got splashed with champagne and whether glass cut people who stood nearby. One fourth of July in Groton (we probably weren't there for two), dad put some firecrackers under a tin can at the bottom of the steep stairs outside the kitchen. The can shot up into the air as the firecrackers went off; I was delighted! In Groton too, dad brought home the brand new 1953 Ford, red and white (with overdrive!); his parents were visiting from Iowa the (Sunday?) my brother and I decided to take our little sister to the park. We couldn't understand why the police had been called and everyone was so upset when we returned hours later. She had, as we anticipated, enjoyed the park very much. Although I don't recall this one, I would guess my brother and I got spankings for that: bare hand (dad's) on bare bottom, over the knee...a favorite form of discipline during the early years.

I attended three schools that year, second grade. My brother and I started in one, then changed when he broke his leg to one with fewer stairs. Then (surprise!) we moved, this time to Monterey, my first introduction to Northern California, my adult home. I finished second grade there before we moved to West Los Angeles, where I got to complete two full years of schooling in the same school! From Monterey, I remember chicken pox and the indelible first seeing of the coast at Big Sur, an enduring adult place of sanctuary and respite. "Cookie," the mutt who was to be my companion and playmate for the next twelve years, joined the family in Monterey, after insistent lobbying on my part. I picked him out of the accidental litter which befell some neighbors and their fenced Scotch terrier; a local boy believed her lonely while in heat and shoved "Cookie's" father over the fence to keep her company. I'm grateful to him; "Cookie" was a good friend, always happy to see me, "so ugly he was cute," smart enough to let us hide and then find us in "hide and seek," the daily alarm clock, always there. My mother and I made the decision to put him to sleep when I was nineteen, visiting on Spring break while a college student. He'd suffered a hernia; surgery would have rendered him a partially immobile, old dog. Until the day of his hernia, his "puppy energy" was intact. I still think we did the right thing by him.

West Los Angeles was the Irish nuns at the Catholic school, my first big crush, on a boy named "Teddy," scares about mom's health due to varicose veins and blood clots, first awareness of my father's touch being somehow not right (with suspicion now that the years of nocturnal fondling had their beginnings at this time or before), a pattern of stealing candy from the corner store, delight in flying kites across the street, neighborhood playmates, Allen next door, Larry up the street, Andrea down. In the back yard we had a huge fig tree which I loved to climb, and plum and apricot trees which bore voluminously. The neighbors gave us avocados from their trees. My brother grew pumpkins (and tomatoes?); I collaborated with Allen next door in a large succulent garden, and we built forts with several rooms from large cardboard boxes. Allen and I discovered and frequently enjoyed secret pre-pubescent sex play; Andrea and I didn't; I remember fondling Larry in his sleep one night when we slept in the same bed at his house. My father and brother were often rageful during our West Los Angeles years; I received beatings from both, my father's both verbal and physical, justified as discipline. My brother was shy, withdrawn, very bright, large for his age. These years, I believe, were the beginnings of his jealousy at my relative social ease and popularity. My father and brother are very good with things, both engineers; I've always been better with people, though there's paradox there as well.

In West LA, I remember well planned and cooked meals, playing croquet as a family in the back yard, a semblance of the "normal" family. We moved again when I was nine, to another part of Los Angeles. What was already in place simply grew. My mother's depression and drinking worsened; she increasingly abdicated her domestic responsibilities. My sister and I took on the shopping and the cooking; in high school (we stayed in the same house for ten years!), if I wanted ironed clothes, I ironed them. Recognition came in the form of being a good bartender (being able to make the perfect martini, and being shown off for this talent to neighbors and friends), while school achievements were pretty much ignored. My father's molestation of me, and I suspect (though he refuses to discuss the subject) my brother, became more overt. His drinking, and rage, increased. The house, the car, the draperies and the carpet were all gray; so were the moods and the souls of the occupants.

We moved a lot because my father was a military officer. Today, even though I've never been in the military, I still move a lot and have all my adult life. It's my experiential norm. Currently, I'm living in a place I love. I've been here less than a year, and wonder constantly where I'll go next. The pattern has receded in scope in recent years, as I've made a commitment to my work and practice as a psychotherapist; I move now within Northern California. Previously, anywhere on the planet was fair game; I've lived and worked in several parts of the world.

Moving was certainly a prime aspect of my childhood — which I carried as learned and familiar behavior into my life as an adult — for which it formed a kind of "bookmark" and habituation; it was simply normal to pick up and move when life invited.

Peter and I moved ten times in our first twenty-five years together; our longest stint was the most recent one in Phoenix (nearly seven years), which almost equals my longest one as a boy, in San Pedro (eight years).

So — new schools, new friends, new neighbors, new climates — leaving the known behind for the unknown, adapting, the family being the only real constant formed the developmental environment that I experienced, oblivious as one is, of the implications of my "normal" being vastly different from that of others — but of course the only one I knew, and therefore perfectly normal to me.

Habituation to moving on — without reservation and seemingly pretty much as a normal activity — also conveniently became a lifelong vehicle for escape and a survival mechanism — as needed.

I mentally catalog memories by where the events took place. The earlier memories are — like everyone's — usually hazier, like dream fragments, the later ones more developed. With time, I understood events more and more in real time;

earlier, things just happened. Today's take on some of the earlier memories, including those described above, follow.

Incubating

Spartan military housing — right on the beach in Cocoa Beach, Florida — was the familial scene I interrupted with my arrival in January 1947. I was born in the base hospital at what was then Banana River Naval Air Station and is now Cape Canaveral.

It was an interruption in the sense that Ken, two and a half at the time, was evidently then experiencing the high point of his childhood — as an only child. As I mentioned earlier, he reportedly soured with resentment at our parents' betrayal when I showed up; an unexpected sharing of the spotlight was not welcome. I of course have no memory of this, but there are photos showing Ken beaming in his so very cute little-boy overalls, eating his almost-too-big-for-him ice-cream cone in this setting. There's another of my father holding me as a very new infant, with more tenderness than I ever remember seeing on his face, sitting on the modest stoop of the family's military-housing apartment, his bare feet in the sand.

Ken's sense of betrayal — and resentment of his baby brother — turned out not to be passing phenomena, so the stage was set there and then for our dynamic as brothers, ours as a family, and Ken's sadly more withdrawn and rarely joyful experience of life.

The La Jolla fire aside, my early memories center around Sharon — and in sharp contrast, my utter delight in having a baby sister. In Wilmington, I remember a large dog biting her in the face and how terrifying that was. She loved animals right from the start, so likely approached or least welcomed the dog — there was no significant scarring, so the episode was perhaps more dramatic in memory than in reality.

Our move to Monterey — where the navy sent my father for a course of study and I completed the second grade — introduces many — more pleasant than not — memories. In addition to my first sight of the Pacific Ocean and convalescing in the dark from measles — all three of us? — Cookie joined the family here — my unrelenting pleadings finally wore my parents down.

My mother returning from house hunting for the next move — to West LA — I think with Ken in tow. This is the last memory I have of her looking radiant, confident, pleased with herself, poised. She was a very attractive woman in her younger years.

The darker ingredients of the stew we all were served over the next several years were no doubt simmering here, but I was blissfully unaware of them at the time.

After Monterey, we rented a house at 2330 Bentley Avenue in West Los Angeles. The houses of that era have all been replaced today with upscale condominiums. My brother's rages started here — he would have been ages ten to twelve during this time — within my father's preferred "zone" for young boys. I shudder to think what might have been happening to him out of the view of others during this time. Still not quite "ripe" myself — to my father's taste — but within range (I was ages seven to nine), I recall bare-hand-on-bare-butt spankings (which in retrospect feels way out of proportion — I was always a well-behaved kid — so likely an excuse for my father) and frequent evening caressing of my butt through my pajamas (ostensibly to make sure I had taken my underwear off — another excuse) but nothing more overt until the next move. He fondled me — us — while we were sleeping during this time.

My brother struck out angrily at me — I of course had no idea why, but he was punished by my father — who had, no doubt in part, caused my brother's acting out — and the distance between us grew.

My mother found me playing with toy cars — a childhood favorite — one day when I had created a mock funeral procession with a note, on top of the hearse/toy van, indicating that the deceased was the (nonexistent) younger brother of my neighbor friend Andrea. She stared, a somber and surprised and somewhat-concerned look on her face — but didn't say anything. I wonder today if, at the time, I wasn't unconsciously recognizing a kind of spiritual death in the world around me.

Chapter Five
San Pedro

San Pedro — where we lived beginning 1956 — the specific neighborhood, today, AKA Palos Verdes Estates — was where things really heated up — and blew up — all over the place. We kids were also older, so could see and understand in ways we had not been able previously. I was ages nine to seventeen during our years there, fifth grade through high school.

Roy and Ellen Ann bought their first house there — for $15,000 — it "Zillows" at just over $1M today. It was a brand-new house in a brand-new development carved out of a hillside just outside of San Pedro. You turned up the hill from Western Avenue on a street called Caddington to get there, and took your first right at the top, on Gunter Road. We were 28639 Gunter Road. The house had hardwood floors, three bedrooms, one and three-quarter baths, and a two-car garage. The houses directly across the street from us had a view out back; we had no view, but had a large backyard in which the folks installed a swimming pool three years later. We were in the first phase of the new development, so got to play in all the open spaces and the subsequent phases of the development when they were under construction.

Ken and I shared a room; Sharon had her own. My birthday is January 3; Ken's was June 29 and Sharon's September 15. I don't recall Ken or I having birthday parties; Sharon did.

Roy was stationed nearby in Long Beach and given his first command in the navy — the USS *Constant* (MSO 427) — an oceangoing minesweeper. Somehow — this seems odd to me now — perhaps a leave before assuming command — but it appeared we had no sooner moved in than he and Ken took off by car for Iowa, ostensibly to visit Roy's parents there. Ken was twelve, "prime" for Roy.

At the time, I was pleased to see them both go away for a while and content to be in our new surroundings with my mother and sister. Roy and Ken drove east in our red-and-white 1953 Ford; the parents bought a wonderful late '40s Packard — like a huge, inverted bathtub — which we three used while the others were away. I loved that car. We went to drive-in movies. Some evenings at the house, we'd have TV dinners — not allowed when Roy was around. I didn't give a second thought to what Ken and Roy might be experiencing on the road, or in Iowa.

Ken returned from his 1956 solo road trip with Roy to Iowa and back even more sullen and withdrawn than before. We shared a room but otherwise kept to ourselves — more or less. One day soon after their return, quite out of the blue, Ken came running into the room we shared, naked and with an erection. I suspect that no one else was home. He moved quickly to cover himself and that was that. I'd love to know the antecedents; there was never a repeat "performance."

Cookie played hide-and-seek with us in that house and was dispatched by my mother to wake us in the morning, which he did dutifully and with delight. Mornings often also began with our parents' flatulent duet echoing off the not-yet-wakened walls of the house. From the outside, I'm sure we looked like any other "normal" White, suburban, post-WWII American family that had newly plopped into the middle class.

We all had chores and were responsible for cleaning our rooms. I remember one time that Roy was doing an "inspection" to see how we had done — probably mostly how I had done since Ken pretty much had abdicated these duties — and he traced his finger across the top of the door jamb. Not surprisingly, he found dust and berated me/us for it. My comment was, "You're my father, not my captain, and I'm your son, not a member of your crew." Startled, he turned and walked away. I'm pretty sure that was the last "inspection."

I was in the Sea Scouts in San Pedro — and we actually had a boat! We sanded it down and got it shipshape and took it out several times — I don't remember how long or how far, but it was fun. We wore sailor uniforms, like our own little play navy. I think Roy was involved as a Scout leader — and likely more, in his twisted, clandestine way — but I was not aware of that at the time.

The Scouts was only one way in which I enjoyed the proximity of the Port of Los Angeles. Chuck and Ivan were two guys — looking back, I'm guessing a couple — who had a fishing boat that they docked in the harbor. I went out fishing with them and remember staying on their boat, and their visiting the house and having drinks with my parents. I always felt safe and cared for by these guys — never a hint of anything inappropriate.

I also spent time in the harbor on my own, free to roam; I remember other friends and other boats. My high school friend Greg and I took a small motorboat — without per-mission — out one evening and cruised around amongst the ships and boats that were docked nearby. Quite fun!

I visited an attractive, slightly older guy on a large sail-boat. I think he might have been the caretaker. I remember one occasion when I was starting up the ladder to the main deck, preparing to leave while he was on the phone, he put his hand on my bare calf and squeezed gently. It was electric, and I wanted to stay, but didn't know what to do, so I left.

I enjoyed sex play there in the harbor — and later at the house (he would sometimes spend the night) — with one of Ken's peers (not friends) named Bob — who I don't think was in the Scouts, so I'm not sure how I knew him. He sometimes let me drive his green-and-white 1950s Oldsmobile, which gave me an erection. I was fourteen or fifteen; he was seven-teen or eighteen. Looking back, Bob seems a good friend to have had, and we had fun together.

The Vincent Thomas Bridge — which linked San Pedro and Terminal Island — where Roy's navy base was located — was constructed during our time in high school, opening to the public in November of my senior year. Curious — and in another example of not completely sound judgment — friends and I decided to drive out onto the bridge (I was, I confess, the driver) toward the end of its construction and before it was operational. We evaded barriers on the San Pedro side and, as I recall, got to at least mid-span before we could not proceed further. So we turned around and retraced our steps. Most manners of mischief and risk-taking were attractive to us.

I had quite a growth spurt in eighth grade — suddenly finding myself at the back of the line when we were arranged by height by the nuns. My voice deepened much earlier than many of my peers, accompanied by wispy facial hair. I became the designated "buyer" in high school — the one of our group most likely not to be carded when buying liquor. Sometimes it worked, and sometimes it didn't.

Some key memories of life in this house take place in the kitchen, or just outside it, at the dining table. In one, Ellen Ann had prepared a turkey for a holiday meal. She had likely been drinking, per usual. When it came time to take the bird out of the oven, she and I alone in the kitchen, she lost her grip on the roasting pan, and the turkey fell and slid halfway across the room on the linoleum floor. I helped her retrieve the errant turkey and get it back into the roasting pan. We cleaned up the floor. She said, "Don't tell your father." I tried not to look at her later as Roy did the carving and passed the plates around, fearing I'd break out laughing.

In another, we were all seated at the table, my father at the head of the table to my left and Sharon to my right. Ken was across from us, and my mother at the end of the table, opposite my father, next to Sharon. Sharon and my father asked for the butter (which was in front of me) at the same time. I started to pass it to my sister when Roy flew into a rage, insisting that this was his house, and he was to be served first. Disgusted, I moved the butter away from Sharon and toward my father, letting it drop in front of him from a couple of inches above the table, saying, "Yes, sir!" Then I excused myself and left the table, saying I had lost my appetite. The others were flabbergasted — one did not confront Roy. Except me — I kind of made a habit of it — he was just a classic bully.

Another one in the kitchen: I was backed up against the washer and dryer, Roy's face red with rage very close to my own, Ellen Ann standing a bit to his left, a few steps back. He accused me of something that hadn't happened, my mother having evidently been the source of the accusation. I calmly told him that what he accused me of had not happened. His rage increased as he yelled, "Are you calling your mother a liar?"

I looked directly at him and said, "No, I'm saying that that didn't happen." He slapped me full force across the face. Ellen Ann looked mortified (she of course knew that she lied — to this day I have no idea why). Continuing to look directly at him, I calmly said, "You can hit me again if you like, but that doesn't change the fact that that didn't happen."

He looked stunned — I think he realized I was telling the truth — and deflated that his authority had been questioned. We all just walked away then, no one speaking further. The undercurrents in that house grew more and more dark and tense.

In another happier dining-table memory there, Sharon and I were eating breakfast one Sunday, only the two of us at the table. The cover of a magazine from the Sunday paper showed a woman making a very funny face, which I had seen and Sharon had not. So, hiding the magazine from Sharon, I turned to her and made the same face at her. She looked puzzled. Then I turned the cover of the magazine toward her, with its funny face alongside my own. She dissolved in hysterics. Ellen Ann was walking past the table at that moment and looked at us with a mixture of amusement and envy at our ease and enjoyment of one another.

San Pedro was where Ellen Ann began to dissolve before our eyes. We'd often catch her staring silently off into space and joke that she was "looking out her window." She took less and less care of herself — wearing a men's white shirt over dark slacks, her hair not formally done for weeks at a time, rather simply brushed back on the sides. She was often in need of a bath.

When we were little, she'd lock us out of the house during the summer and stay inside alone. She suffered pervasive anhedonia and abdicated household tasks like shopping, cooking, and ironing — in addition to picking up her liquor — to us kids as we got older. More below on this one. She'd visit with a neighbor across the street, Julie, who was also a confidante. She was often sad — severely depressed, I recognize now — and barely present.

We were all given the choice to attend public or Catholic schools. I was the only one who chose Catholic, and stuck with that from fifth grade all the way through college. I had wanted to go into the seminary after eighth grade, but my parents said I was too young to make that decision. I was disappointed at the time, but they were right; I went in after high school instead — and lasted ten days. More on that below.

In grammar school, one day at recess, I was running with the ball, and our coach realized that I was really fast — I had no idea — and that led to my joining the track team in high school, a blessing, since I was otherwise a bit too bookish to fit in with the "cool" kids.

In seventh grade, it was my turn. I was twelve; it was 1959 — the same year Roy retired from the navy — and my father invited me to spend time with him on his ship, docked then in San Diego — an unusual, but welcome in its way, invitation — and hugely transformative.

The prior year, commander now of an entire division of minesweepers, he had contracted hepatitis while in the Far East. The USS *Prestige*, in his division, ran aground in Japan. Another of his ships, the USS *Pivot*, was damaged trying to get the *Prestige* off the rocks, without success. The *Prestige* was declared a total loss and blown up.

During this same trip, Roy was hospitalized overseas with hepatitis and jaundice. He was court-martialed later as the senior officer at the time of the grounding. He was cleared of responsibility for the accident, but I believe that those in command of the *Prestige* were found to have been responsible. We of course worried about him as a family the entire time. So in this context, his invitation and attention were welcome, particularly given that the period of his absence had been an especially dark one at home, with Ken at war with our mother, and her unable to control him.

In one instance, Ken came storming in a rage into our shared room, picked up a good-sized plaster piggy bank that I had on the dresser, and shattered it against the wall, then broke a wooden hanger over Ellen Ann when she tried to discipline him, which caused her to faint. He simply stepped detachedly over her slumped there on the floor in the entry, then walked over, sat down, and turned on the TV. It was left to me to tend to her. I was maybe eleven, so Sharon was seven or eight. When she came to, I asked her if she was OK — she said that her heart was broken and not to tell Roy.

In Roy's stateroom, one day during my time with him on his flagship as division commander, he laid me out on his bunk and masturbated me. His face was grotesque, distorted by lust; I had never seen such an expression.

There had been an earlier incident at the house; he took me into the bathroom and closed the door. Everyone else was home. Here, too, he laid me out — on the counter — and pulled down my pants, hungrily examining my genitals. He might have said something like "I just wanted to see how developed you are now." I had to have been prepubescent, but was not buying that at all. It was just weird.

In his stateroom, I was uncomfortable and not sure what he was doing or why. It was my first orgasm; it surprised me — and I knew it should have been a private moment — which I would never have chosen to share with him. He cleaned me up and told me that was something I should not do on my own (fat chance).

Moments later, we were in the officers' wardroom at lunch. He was the senior officer — and had just molested his son in his cabin. He carried on as if nothing was different; for me, nothing would ever be the same. Looking back, I am stunned at his shamelessness and ability to compartmentalize.

In both instances, while I needed a loving and protecting father, he wanted sexual gratification…from his own son. His wants trumped my needs; if I wished to find a healthy role model, adult nurturance and protection, and positive mirroring, I would have to find it elsewhere.

Sadly, this is exactly the dynamic that makes trauma/abuse victims so vulnerable to predators: our unmet needs continue seeking to be met; our ability to distinguish genuine interest and affection from manipulation is impaired by our earlier experiences.

After the incident on the ship, he tried to molest me further, but I would not allow it. One day, just the two of us in the house, he chased me around with an obvious erection showing in his pants; I fought him off and ran outside until someone else came home. I was mortified, terrified, furious — and trapped.

Meanwhile, I was student body president, getting straight As and lettering in two sports.

What options does a teenage kid have in such a situation? I thought of running away — several times — this was one of those instances. One fantasy was that I would go to New Orleans and become a drummer in a jazz band; it's a good thing that I didn't pursue that one, as I later learned that I have virtually no musical talent at all. Bottom line: I was too scared, didn't want to abandon my sister — and actually liked other parts of my life. So I decided to stick it out and leave at the first opportunity, hoping for a less drastic path to emerge.

So, that evening, we sat at the dinner table as we always did. Sitting next to my father, privately seething, I was silent and alone with my rage and my secret...again. I hated him.

To this day, it amazes me that he thought that he could or would ever again have any sort of moral authority over me. Instead, he made all authority figures suspect in my eyes, and I determined that respect was to be granted only when earned. Little could I know or understand then the affinity and affection I felt years later for young men who had run away — or been cast out — and lived their damaged lives on the streets.

Already self-conscious as a newly pubescent, barely budding early adolescent, I had "molestation by my father" to add to my other developmental tasks and challenges, which included body image, sexuality, a certainty that the whole world was as conscious of my appearance as I was, and an abiding fear that they could look at me and see that I harbored a dark secret...or two. Herewith was born my lifelong private stew of who and how to be socially and sexually in the world.

Social anxiety became a prominent part of my personality, which puzzled others when they witnessed it: a poised and confident young man whose façade could crumble in an instant.

It took me decades to be able to sleep with my back to the door — a response to his habit of sneaking in and fondling me in my sleep.

When I was in high school, I had friends over — for a while. On one occasion, he goosed one friend of mine as he was walking out the door with others — no attempt to be subtle in the least. This was not a casual grazing of my friend's butt; this was a grab-a-cheek-and-hold-on event. We were all so stunned that no one spoke. I was, again, absolutely mortified...and ashamed.

In time, I learned which friends he was not attracted to and invited only them over — but not frequently. The man was totally out of control.

At the same time — a bit of Jekyll and Hyde — a London friend and colleague, who met Roy when he visited me in London after Ellen Ann died, found him "absolutely charming" — even though he knew what our history had been. I learned later that this is a not-uncommon duality of sociopaths.

Fermin Lasuen High School sat on a bluff across town, above the Pacific Ocean. It was difficult not to daydream looking out the classroom windows at the sea. I was an A student, ran track well, played poorly on the school tennis team, acted convincingly enough in the cast of *Oklahoma* (which the drama teacher thanked me for, helping as a more popular kid to normalize this activity), competed well in speech tournaments — was even invited to serve as a judge for some — and was elected student body president. I had girlfriends...and a number of unrequited crushes on my male classmates. I was never "football-team popular," but my teachers and peers pretty much all seemed to like me well enough.

Few were aware that anything was amiss with my family. One didn't in those days think or speak — and there was virtually no public awareness — of domestic violence, sexual abuse within the family, alcoholic parents, etc. It wouldn't have occurred to me to confide in a teacher — or priest — about such things. As long as the family's public face, veneer of normalcy, was maintained, all was well with the world.

So, my "hero" mask firmly in place, I went about my day-to-day. The parents of one close friend, who thought my parents overly strict, would frequently lie or cover for me so that I could enjoy greater freedoms than I would have otherwise. But I recall there being no indication that they suspected that anything was otherwise out of the ordinary. I don't recall experiencing depression during these years, but was highly anxious, aware that I harbored secrets, that I was different from my peers, and that I frequently didn't know how to act in public.

When I was fourteen, my mother lamented my unending enthusiasm for trying new things. "If we let you do everything you want to do now, what's going to be left?" she asked one day. I was and am flabbergasted by this sentiment as — to my view then and now — the well has no bottom.

A few years later, my father noted, upon my return from a speech tournament or leadership conference or some such, "You always come home with a new job," a committee assignment or leadership position. "When is enough enough?" he asked. Very revealing.

I had my first paying job — and my second — while the family lived in San Pedro. The first when I was fifteen — washing dishes in a small restaurant — the first of MANY restaurant jobs over the years, a sector that became a kind of second home for me, always there when I needed it — was owned by a gruff, older Greek man (whom I became very fond of) and was located just down the road from my high school. My parents had to drive me to work. The second I walked to — bagging groceries at the new supermarket that had been built in a previously virgin field down the road from where we lived, just off Caddington. Here was where my mother befriended the manager of the liquor department; he would accept a note and cash from her as sufficient to send me home with a bottle of cheap gin or vodka — quite embarrassing for a high school kid who worked in the same store.

My mother had been quite athletic when she was younger, but never as I knew her. I've never — to this day — considered myself much of an athlete, but since I was the only one in our family who was the least bit athletically inclined, I was officially the athlete in the family. I did, in fairness, also acquire a love of downhill skiing — in the French Alps — during the London years. This has meaning to the tale only insofar as it fueled jealousy on my father's part and likely deepened the chasm of disaffinity with my brother.

My San Pedro friend Joe had a gloriously restored and loved-to-death '30s or '40s bright-orange pickup truck. He'd drive to the beach — usually Redondo — in the summer, and we'd ride in the back, body surf, get too much sun, ride home again in the back...and look forward to the next time. One time, he dropped me off a minute or two past the deadline to be home Roy had set for me that day; I was grounded for the next week, even though I had no control over the situation.

Roy could often be an asshole like that, some kind of sick power trip, totally unnecessary. I've always been a "spirit of the law" guy myself — a good intention and "close enough" works just fine in my book.

Our high school locker room was a converted classroom, a wall of six or eight showerheads at one end, lockers against the other walls, and benches in between — all open, no stalls or partitions. PE, practice, and home matches/meets all started and ended in this room — with a delightful multitude of naked and half-naked guys, many wet. You could look only if you pretended not to, and definitely no touching — except accidental bumping into, towel snapping, butt slapping, etc. The brawny football players ruled the roost, and the poor scrawny and pudgy guys who were in the chess club and worked on the yearbook cowered and tried their best to be invisible. I was somewhere in between. It was an exhilarating kind of torture.

My sexual development was already garbled because of my father, and it was an era when one could absolutely not acknowledge same-sex attractions. The Stonewall Riots and the emergence of a visible gay culture were still years away. So I was dating girls — which on some level I knew was unfair and dishonest, while a part of me hoped it was not.

I learned to compartmentalize and act; I kept my confusion and real feelings — to the extent that I understood them — to myself, well hidden. The stage was set. Knocked off the track of any "normal" chronological psychosexual development, the years that followed were marked by continuing fragmentation and confusion; generous amounts of Catholic guilt; "boundary," trust, and identity issues; and living a double life, personally and professionally — with accompanying shame, guilt, and depression; a sense of isolation, and periods of helplessness that these disparate elements of self would never come together into a coherent whole.

Meanwhile, the world around me acquired an electric, hypersexual aspect that did not make matters any better whatsoever. I in turn became hypervigilant both to any new threats — and to any possibility of giving away my secrets.

In other words, I didn't get to discover sex and my own sexuality on my own, in an age-appropriate fashion, in concert with my peers. That was taken from me — mostly by my father, but also by the larger society at the time — and could never be returned. It's a wound, insult, and interruption that impacts an entire life; one can only do the best one can afterwards — and hope not to hurt others along the way.

There was to be a very painful and perplexing decade — literally ten full years — between my first orgasm, delivered at my father's hand in the stateroom of his ship, and my first experience of intercourse with a hippie girl named Lisa — in a motel room in Big Sur, with a friend Dennis playing guitar throughout the brief but powerful exchange — and another guy whose identity I cannot remember there as well — perhaps pretending to sleep?

My high school girlfriend April and I had a lot of fun together — we'd drive up to LAX and watch people getting off planes greet the people waiting for them. It was pre 9/11 of course, so there were no security barriers. Sometimes we'd pretend that one of us had just arrived, and the other was the greeter. We'd drive up to Hollywood and ogle the crowds outside of movie premieres, in awe of the searchlights and movie stars arriving in their fancy cars. We'd sometimes double-date with April's best friend, Linda, and her boyfriend, Steve (major crush). Sometimes we'd park and neck, April and I in the back seat. I'd always imagine Steve beside me in her place.

Ours was the second graduating class from Fermin Lasuen, which was closed for financial reasons after only a decade or so. The Bay of Pigs debacle occurred in the spring of our freshman year. JFK was assassinated in November of our senior year; the Beatles arrived in the USA the following spring, just weeks before our graduation.

My friends and I mercilessly teased Ken during this time, calling him Carrot. He was tall and lanky with a large mop of curly, dark hair. He was also scary smart, with an amazing vocabulary — even compared with a highly educated adult — and was socially very withdrawn. He preferred the company of adults; he spent his lunchtimes in high school playing bridge with teachers, and frequently lost himself in science fiction — the only serious reader in the household.

Today, we'd likely see him as somewhere on the autism spectrum — then he was something of a freak to us, and given his and my history and my ignorance of its roots, I was not inclined to be kind to him. I was a fairly popular, fun-loving adolescent with lots of friends; we could not have been more opposite.

Sharon was always shy, even as a child. She was also incredibly tough…and stubborn. She was the baby and the only girl; my impulse was always to protect her. We used to tease and play as siblings; she had a good neighbor friend across the street.

Ellen Ann was a terrible role model and often unkind toward Sharon — perhaps replaying her relationship with her own mother.

As I mentioned earlier, Roy would delight in telling people that I "didn't know which end of a screwdriver to pick up" — he did have a point, but this was more than a slight exaggeration. He visited once when I had just settled into a new condominium on the Carquinez Strait in Vallejo. I had friends to dinner when he was there, and he remarked at one point that he could tell us where every joist and pipe and electrical line was behind the closed walls. I responded that I could do the same thing with people. Touche!

There was one very rare occasion when I was left alone in the San Pedro house for a weekend — I can't imagine or remember how that happened. But what does a precocious high school boy left home alone do? Party!! It started with inviting a few friends over, then a few acquaintances…then the word spread, and that night the neighborhood streets were lined up and down with cars. The house was crammed full, mostly with people I did not know and had never seen before; there was at least one fight. Someone dropped a cigarette in my parents' bedroom. Much beer was consumed. There was breakage, but no one and no debris wound up in the pool.

I remember going from a nervous excitement to terror as the crowd grew; I spent the evening doing damage control. My closer friends and I cleaned up and covered up as best we could, but there was no way I was going to get away with it. My parents' reaction is a bit fuzzy to me today — I think they were somewhat stunned, and I suspect I was grounded at the very least. Our neighbors were certainly all aware of this gathering. Fortunately, we were able to obscure some of the more damaging details. It was my first and last home-alone party.

In another, far more benign home-alone moment — this one at Greg's grandparents' house when no one was supposed to be home — four or five of us decided to go skinny-dipping one evening in the pool. I may have been the instigator here as well. Imagine our surprise when — all of us naked and in the water — the lights came on in the house and pool, and Greg's grandmother appeared on the upstairs balcony. I remember hugging the wall closest to the house, Greg alongside me. This wound up being an incident in which there was more residual bemusement than anything else, and all had a good story to tell. I was quite enjoying myself before those damn lights came on.

I had otherwise and mostly been a dutiful kid around the house. I washed the cars, mowed the lawn, and cleaned the pool — always earning my allowance.

One weekend morning at the San Pedro house, Ellen Ann and we kids, all recovering from the flu, had a surprise visitor — a boyishly handsome young sailor named Fred from my father's ship. It turned out that we had the same birthday; he was a nice guy, as I recall. We were in our pajamas, and the house was a mess, so we were all embarrassed, and it was very awkward. Roy, however, was delighted to see the young man and had clearly invited him to visit — without telling the others. At Christmastime, Roy and I drove over to Fred's apartment to leave gifts for him and his wife and child.

Even I knew at the time that this was a highly unorthodox relationship, from both a military and a familial perspective. Years later, in a moment of rare but occasional candor, Roy confessed to me that he and Fred had been having an affair — shocker! — and that Fred would "spring an erection when he saw me headed his way." So the navy commander was shamelessly molesting his children at home while happily engaged in a hugely inappropriate sexual relationship with an also-married subordinate and member of his crew. Is it any wonder that figuring out appropriate boundaries was such a life task for me?

Years later, there was another boy/young man named Fred who played a hugely consequential role in Roy and Ellen Ann's life — details to follow.

One day, at the San Pedro house, in a rare moment of insight and concern, Roy asked me why I seemed always anxious to be away from the house. I was away at every possible moment, including taking long solo drives around the Palos Verdes peninsula. I looked at him and said simply, "Because it's not a very happy place to be." His ability to not see or recognize the effects of his own behavior on his family is staggering, even now in memory.

It was a strict household — in which I did manage, in retrospect, quite a lot of freedom. My friend Mike's family had a family friend, Cassie, who, with her husband/partner, had a cabin in Big Bear, where she would host four of five of us for a week or so in the summer. The last time, we somehow had the school's cheerleading megaphone with us — and my friend John unfortunately had a red 1956 Ford. The red Ford, the megaphone, and a group of immature high school boys — sad to say, I was likely in the lead — turned out to be a very bad mix in this always very-dry-in-summer mountain community.

For some reason, we thought it would be clever and fun to drive through neighborhoods, exclaiming through the megaphone that everyone should evacuate because a large fire was headed their way. What in the world were we thinking?!

Not surprisingly, it didn't end well — our parents and Cassie had to accompany us later to a court appearance, where the judge kindly let us off with a warning, given that we were genuinely remorseful and clearly "good boys" who had no record of other stupid behavior. Neither the parents nor Cassie were amused. To the extent that I was the ringleader, my friends' parents encouraged some distance between their sons and me after that incident — though I don't recall our friendships suffering.

Not my proudest moment — I can't help making the connection today between the fire of my earliest memory and the bizarre decision to terrify these good people with the possibility of one of their own.

Roy retired from the US Navy in 1959, when I was twelve and we were living in San Pedro, as lieutenant commander — a mid-level junior officer — after twenty-two years of service, having been passed over for promotion. I've always wondered if the navy got wind of his secret life.

Ken graduated from San Pedro High School in 1962 and enrolled as a student at UCLA that fall. Having by then amassed multiple master points as a champion bridge player while at UCLA, and attempting to forge his grades since he rarely attended classes, Ken was expelled from UCLA in 1963. I was assigned the task of driving up to UCLA and collecting him and his belongings. In early 1964, on my seventeenth birthday, Roy dug out his old uniform and swore Ken into the US Navy — best birthday present ever!

Ken retired in 1990, also as lieutenant commander, with Sharon, Roy, and me in attendance. More to tell on that a bit later.

I got my driver's license at sixteen in 1963. The freedom was exhilarating. I didn't mind the errands and chauffeur duties at all.

Most fun of all was driving Roy's used 1960 Austin-Healey 3000 when he was away on business travel. Ken was in the Navy; Sharon was too young to drive, and Ellen was afraid of this car — I was not! Getting up to 110 mph on the Pasadena Freeway seemed very cool at the time, albeit a bit unwise from my current perspective. Envious attention was guaranteed with every sortie in this car — from girls and boys alike!

Eventually, this wonderful toy had to go due to Roy's multiple speeding tickets. It was replaced by a HUGE 1960 Cadillac sedan — a bit of keeping up with the neighborhood Joneses — which Roy was initially intimidated by; I drove it home the first day. Sharon, who was all of five feet tall, could barely see over its dash. Ellen drove — but did not love — this car. I thought it was fun as well — in a different way from the Austin-Healey. There was room in this boat for lots of people!

San Pedro launched each of us and all of us as a family in a variety of ways. This was where Roy and Ellen bought their first house. As inevitably happens, the kids grow up and leave home, beginning the journey of finding their own way in the larger world...and the spousal relationship evolves.

Sharon got uprooted her last year of high school when Roy and Ellen moved to Anaheim in 1967 to be closer to Roy's new job as an engineering writer for Hughes Aircraft. Always shy, Sharon had to leave her few childhood friends behind and enter a time and a home in which it was just her and the parents — alone. She graduated from high school there in 1968.

On one relatively rare visit to the family physician, shortly after I was ushered into his office, he began to upbraid me about my behavior toward my mother. I told him he had me confused with my brother — but learned that my mother was at least confiding in someone.

Ellen's transition was more internal than external. San Pedro was the first house where Roy and Ellen slept in separate beds in the same room. As her nest emptied — and already not the most engaged parent — she drank more, and her depression deepened. She paid less and less attention to her appearance. It's hard to imagine that she was entirely unaware that her husband was molesting at least two of their children — and who knows how many outside the family. She joined with Roy in drinking, farting, and being angry — though hers was always less intense and enduring than Roy's — at least in the latter two categories.

She used to call me "boy" — even when I was older — in a very affectionate manner. Just me — it felt like something special between us.

Even Cookie left us in San Pedro — his twelve-year puppy-hood came to a sudden end with a hernia, for which Ellen Ann made the decision not to operate. I was home from college. The parents sent Sharon and me off to see a movie in an attempt to ease our grief. He had been a godsend, lifesaver, and dear friend throughout my childhood, and his loss was deeply felt. I remember him fondly and well today.

Part II

Escape — and
Swimming in It

Chapter Six
Men of the Cloth

Four of us high school buddies set out one day in my parents' older Austin sedan for Northern California, to visit college campuses, since we were all then considering where we wanted to apply. I'm guessing we were juniors. We got as far as Solvang, where the Austin blew a rod. Roy was furious at me (of course) and had to come collect us and deal with his broken car. End of college tour.

We had multiple college recruiters visit us at Fermin Lasuen during our junior and senior years, especially from the Catholic colleges and universities. One of the more memorable to me was a Christian Brother named Brother Albert Rahill, former president of Saint Mary's College of California (SMC) in the 1930s — when it was a football powerhouse. He was a diminutive man with a shock of white hair and an immediately endearing twinkle in his eye.

I could have in no way predicted it that day, but he became a friend. The Christian Brothers, founded in France in the seventeenth century, were the first Roman Catholic congregation of male nonclerics devoted solely to schools, learning, and teaching.

I applied to Stanford (denied), and received acceptances from USC, Santa Clara, Holy Cross (a favor to my mother, who wanted me to at least consider her Massachusetts and her New England) — and SMC. My parents wanted me to live at home for college, and offered to buy me "any car you want" if I did so. VERY clear that I needed to escape at the first possible opportunity, I told them simply that I didn't need a car. Prior to leaving home for college, my only escapes had been either to retreat inside myself, behind my mask, or to venture out for long solitary drives — just to get away. This was my first opportunity to escape the family in a major way, and I did not hesitate to take it — even though it meant leaving Sharon on her own with our parents.

In fall 1964, at seventeen, I entered the seminary for the Oblates of Mary Immaculate (the priests who taught at Lasuen) — in Lafayette, SF East Bay, Northern California — and enrolled with the other seminarians as a day student at SMC, in nearby Moraga. Several of my high school class-mates were also attending SMC as freshmen lay students.

Packed inextricably, shamefully, and invisibly away in my baggage as I set out, of course, was the jumble of my being in that moment a "survivor" (a term that was not in use at the time) of both incest and an alcoholic, physically abusive, and severely distressed family…together with my not-at-all-yet sorted-out sexual orientation, in an era when homosexuality was considered sinful, criminal, and a psychi-atric disorder. Catholic teachings were not particularly helpful on the latter issue.

My stay at the seminary lasted a brief ten days, but I spent the next four years at SMC — which I would likely not have attended in the first place had it not been for the seminary.

94

My roommate at the seminary had been a seminarian since eighth grade. He changed his clothes in the closet and believed in strict observance of the rules. We were not allowed to snack between meals; I mentioned to him that, in my desk drawer, I had a secret stash of candy, which he was welcome to share. He said that was against the rules.

We were awakened each morning by the unpleasant clanging of a handbell in the hallway outside our rooms. We read Scripture to one another at meals — there were maybe a dozen of us. One hot afternoon, I started out the door for mandatory recreation, shirtless and in only gym shorts and tennis shoes. I was told to go back inside and cover my body since that attire was indecent. I was astonished; I had just been a fun-in-the-sun, beach-loving Southern California boy — this all seemed really bizarre and a tad unhealthy.

My doubts about remaining at the seminary started almost immediately. I confessed them in a phone call with my parents, and they suggested I talk with the Father Superior — the guy in charge. I found him on his putting green behind the priests' residence. I told him I wasn't sure this was going to work for me. Without looking up from his putt, he said I'd get a full refund and to arrange my departure when the others were not around.

Bolstered by this excellent spiritual guidance, I did as requested. At the college, I moved in with my Lasuen classmate Frank, in Assumption Hall...intending to transfer to another school at the first opportunity. But I stayed. My parents paid for tuition, room and board, a total of about $25K, I believe, and I did odd jobs in the area — pulling weeds, painting sheds, etc. — through the campus employment office for play money and incidentals.

Sandwiched between my A averages in high school and graduate school were my more average "gentleman's Cs" at SMC. I majored in English — deciding against psychology after one class in which the instructor had us draw a human figure, then walked around observing us as we drew — I felt completely naked — and discovered my love for fiction.

We drank copious amounts of beer at our off-campus weekend keggers; I loved the occasional food fights that followed in the dining commons — in the best ones, you could barely see the ceiling for all the food in the air.

I was probably an episodic binge drinker at SMC — the closest I've been in my life to what I would today consider being an alcoholic. At the same time, it was purely social/recreational — there was never any solitary drinking, nor daily drinking or hidden drinking, etc. It was, I think — though often unquestionably to excess — to fit in, what we college boys all did when together.

I had little or no insight into the dynamics or more nuanced aspects of alcoholism at the time, but did understand that if I wanted my parents to remember a phone conversation from SMC, I needed to call during the day, since evening conversations were not remembered the next day...which could at the same time be handy in a CYA kind of way if there was news to deliver that was best not remembered.

Adding to the mix and alcoholic permissions of those years, the Christian Brothers had their own winery in Napa Valley...so wine and brandy were plentiful on campus.

I got to know Brother Albert well when I joined the external circuit of alumni and other social events as a presentable, articulate class and student body president. I often accompanied

Albert to such events — including, notably, SMC alum and great Albert friend Joe Alioto's inauguration as mayor of San Francisco in January of 1968.

After we got to know one another, Albert would occasionally call me in the dorm in the evening (we had a shared pay phone in the hall at the time — one per floor — no phones in our rooms — way before personal cell phones) and suggest that I come over to his office to discuss some weighty matter of state or another. A bottle of Christian Brothers brandy and several hours later, we'd bid one another good night and retire to our respective domiciles.

I missed several early morning classes after these evenings with Albert, but wouldn't trade them for the world. I came to love the man, and enjoyed my time with him immensely. There was never anything the least bit creepy or inappropriate about Albert or our time together. He wasn't a father figure, nor an authority figure. We simply became friends, despite the nearly fifty-year age gap. He was the first person to tell me that I had a good mind; he urged me to put it to good use.

I enjoyed teasing Albert, and he enjoyed being teased — and loved to tease as well. At one alumni event in San Francisco, celebrating what may have been the centennial anniversary of the order's arrival in the USA, Albert and I were amongst those seated at the head table. When I was asked to speak, I commented that we were honored to have with us that evening one of the original arrivals, and asked Albert to stand. He did — twinkle-eyed — to rapturous applause. I knew he would get me back, and looked forward to that.

The Christian Brothers also operated Manhattan College in New York. One summer, three of us SMC students were in NYC for a conference of some sort, and Albert happened to be staying at Manhattan College. We agreed to meet up one morning, and Albert suggested a short stroll down the hill to a bar he knew would be open — for a drink.

Albert was one of the very few truly saintly people I have ever encountered.

SMC was all male at the time — it became coed years later. On weekends, we dated girls from Holy Names in Oakland and Dominican in San Rafael. My most serious and regular girlfriend during this time, Mary, attended Dominican — and the Richmond-San Rafael Bridge became very familiar.

My classmate crushes were excruciating, multiple, and unrequited. In the dorms, we showered in large open rooms — ghosts of the locker room at Lasuen. During our freshman "initiation," an upperclassman came around to our rooms with a ruler to measure our dicks — oddly, something all seemed to take in stride. For better or worse, I was out when he came to our room; I'm not sure how I would have reacted.

A small group of us engineered a daring commando raid wherein we hung a pro-SMC/anti-arch rival USF banner across the east tunnel entrance in the middle of the Bay Bridge — complete with a fake flat tire, lookouts, and pre-stunt reconnaissance. Later, we interrupted an attempted sneak-attack reprisal at the edge of our campus and apprehended and shaved the heads of the perpetrators.

The Air Force sent some recruiters to campus one time and positioned an engineless combat jet at the entrance to campus to announce their presence. One night, a group of us decided to move it over in front of the dorms. Though the recruiters were likely impressed, they were not amused, and the college administration was both irked and embarrassed.

Ah well, boys will be boys; it was all great fun.

On a few occasions, when we happened to be sharing a bed off campus, I fondled sleeping classmates — a learned clandestine behavior, carried over from boyhood, and contributing factor to the profound shame in which my adolescent and early-adult sexuality were so tightly wrapped. It took me years to understand and unlearn this pernicious behavior with which I "stole" from another as I had been stolen from by my father. It shames me today to think of it.

On one occasion, I was the recipient — a guy I didn't really know, the date of a friend of Mary's, on an occasion when the girls slept in one room and the boys in another — good Catholic kids. After a night out in San Francisco, he and I happened to share a bed. It was like being back on that boat in San Pedro — electric and confusing. I knew I liked what he was doing, but didn't know what to do, so pretended to sleep.

As we classmates got to know one another, we of course visited one another's lives, homes, and families. One roommate and good friend, Tom, was from a prominent agricultural family in the Oxnard area; his father once flew us back to campus in his small private plane. Another classmate took us sailing on the San Francisco Bay in the family sailboat. On one outing, I nudged poor Mary so that she fell overboard. I was trying to be funny, but no one — including me eventually — saw the humor. She was particularly not amused. The bay's waters are cold and currents strong. It was a really,

really stupid thing to do. My late-adolescent judgment was no better than it had been earlier on.

One morning during a visit in the Central Valley, a classmate's mother served us a delectable breakfast of scrambled eggs with lots of fresh ingredients and side dishes. Both my friend and she were startled at how much I acclaimed the meal, an ordinary occurrence for them. Little did they know that such things had long ceased happening in the King household. Years prior, when the subject of scrambled eggs for breakfast was raised at home, Ellen Ann said, "Only if you wash the pan."

One time, an SMC friend whose family I had come to know was in a minor car accident. He asked me to call his parents to tell them that he was mildly hurt and being tended to, but OK. I was struck that they dropped everything and raced to the hospital to be with him.

By contrast, I was driving a borrowed Chevy Corvair one weekend, three friends on board, up in the hills near campus. I took a curve too quickly, and the car rolled (uphill, fortunately — there was a sharp drop on the other side of the road); we landed upside down, pointing in the opposite direction from the one we had been traveling. There was a moment of awful silence, all four of us more or less crumpled together inside on the roof of the inverted vehicle. I broke the silence by asking if everyone was OK, fearing of course that they were not. One by one, each checked in and said they were OK. One voice from the back seat said, "Turn the motor off." Dave, who had been in the passenger's seat, remembered, more than fifty years later, that the wheels were still spinning when he climbed out of the upturned vehicle.

I had hit the windshield with my head, which made a spiderweb effect in the glass, and (I learned later) compressed some lower vertebrae, causing a small fracture — which occasioned a lifetime of back pain — ongoing. When I called home to report the incident, Roy was angry that I had damaged the car. Only when my mother came on the phone was I asked if we were all OK. Very fortunately, none of the others had significant injuries.

When I sought medical advice on the injury, I was offered the option of surgery — or simply learning to live with it and adjust my activities accordingly. I chose the latter, feeling that back surgery was too risky to entertain. Interestingly, looking back, my parents were not involved in this decision. It's a decision I don't regret today, as the pain has been manageable. I was an avid downhill skier for years, and learned to manage the discomfort during long flights as I traveled around the world.

Much less fortunately, in the great tragedy of my years at SMC, some friends went out for a drive on a beautiful spring Sunday. I was invited, but elected to stay behind. They accidentally drove off a curvy road in Tilden Park, throwing my good friend Tom (different Tom from my roommate) out of the car, which subsequently landed on him as it rolled down the hill. Tom was killed instantly; the others sustained minor injuries. We all were stunned when word reached campus. I was devastated — we were close friends, and this was my first experience of a peer's death.

I went to the coroner's office in downtown Oakland to be there when Tom's mother arrived. His parents were divorced, so I knew she would be on her own. Later, evening now,

I returned to the college and a chapel full of Tom's many friends who had gathered to pray for him and his family.

Tom was a dear and special friend, charming, witty, bright, and fun. We saw the world differently — he more conservatively/traditionally than I. We respected one another as people and agreed to learn from one another in order to better understand the other's perspective. I enjoyed watching him play rugby, and he enjoyed my being amongst the spectators.

We double-dated. One evening, dropping off our dates at Dominican, I was at the top of an internal staircase, saying good night to Mary, and Tom was below, on the ground level, out of Mary's sight. He had already bid his date good night. Suddenly, echoing loudly off the stairwell walls, came a mighty fart. I looked over the railing to see Tom doubled over in laughter, quite pleased with himself.

Tom was beloved by all who knew him. As a class gift to the college, we commissioned a life-sized bronze Madonna and Child and dedicated it to his memory. It was placed before a small pool in the new library. I spent quite a lot of time, in the years after, with Tom's mother, Maggie, and his younger brother, Jim. Jim — years later — asked me if Tom and I had been lovers. We had not — not even a hint of anything sexual, but our closeness was obviously apparent, and I took Jim's question as a compliment to our friendship.

Maggie gave me a small volume of St. Thomas's *My Way of Life*, which she had inscribed and given to Tom when he went off to college. I have and treasure it today — and of course miss Tom and wonder who he would have become. Maggie took a job in a local mortuary after Tom's death — knowing she would understand people's pain and confusion, and helping herself heal in the process. She is no longer with us.

Overall, what struck me most about visiting classmates' families was the warmth and richness of their home life and how much their families clearly cherished them. I envied the planet they lived on.

It was the sixties (1964–1968), and it was the San Francisco Bay Area during the Vietnam War. Martin Luther King was assassinated in April of our senior year; Robert Kennedy was assassinated two months later, just days before we graduated.

My first time smoking weed was as a senior at SMC, with three junior friends, on a camping trip to Big Sur — where we slept on the beach, smoked joints they had brought (getting Neal stoned for the first time was a part of the trip's agenda), and watched all the pretty colors change in the sky and sea at sunset. After that trip, friends and I smoked weed in the student council offices on campus with alacrity, the deviant/forbidden aspect of it adding to the enjoyment.

There was a fascinating, almost-generational divide at this moment in time. Most of my classmates and those older than us did not smoke weed or identify with the emerging social and cultural upheaval going on all around us; a few from my class and many in the classes a year or two behind us embraced it all with curiosity and enthusiasm.

I was honored by my peers in being elected both class and student body president. I was the first student member of the board of trustees appointed by the college president, Brother Michael, a Christian Brother and the first psychologist I had ever known personally. Michael had participated in the early Civil Rights demonstrations and marches in Washington and the South, which I found both laudable and impressive.

One evening, while drinks were being served in the president's dining room before a trustee dinner, I was chatting with him and a friend of mine. I handed him a baggie of weed (we had talked earlier about my having tried it, and he was curious). After a brief moment of surprise and uncertainty, he realized what it was and stuffed it quickly into a pocket in his robes. The evening proceeded, the three of us aware of what he had hidden in his robes. That was a fun moment.

Michael and I also enjoyed evenings — and often a drink or two — in his office. I confided in him, and he, in time, confided in me. I talked with him about my family, my abuse history, and my confused and contorted sexuality. He once told me that he became a monk partly to avoid the military and being in such proximity to other young men. As far as I knew then, he had taken his vow of celibacy literally. I came to consider him to be a friend as well, but more complicatedly than Albert, given his position of authority and our personal confidences.

Michael was overweight, and his physician once put him on a grapefruit diet. Michael said that there was no prohibition — that he was aware of — to adding gin to his grapefruit juice, so that was his diet drink. I don't think he lost much weight.

Again, everyone seemed to like me well enough, though not all were entirely at ease with the persona I presented. My many moments of social awkwardness stood in sharp contrast to the more composed and confident young man most saw in the day-to-day. One dorm counselor called me an enigma; I liked that. A dorm mate down the hall asked me once, "Are you queer?" I think I just walked away, inwardly terrified that he had "seen" me. Some intuited or even glimpsed behind my mask, but I doubt any saw so deeply as the terrified, unloved, and abandoned little boy that I carried inside.

Many were of course sexually active; I was not. While it was somewhat easy to hide behind being a "good Catholic boy," my celibacy was also not 100-percent convincing — and was suspect. My girlfriend went along, tolerated. I was of course confused and tortured internally, at the same time, and severely compartmentalized. How I would love to have had a secret boyfriend during those SMC years — someone with whom to have navigated the confusion and loneliness.

One evening, walking across campus with friends, the most remarkable voice pierced the darkness, wafting from a concert by Big Brother and the Holding Company that evening in the college gym. That was my first exposure to Janis Joplin. My prior experience of singing at SMC was almost entirely endless choruses of "The Bells of Saint Mary's" sung in ragged beer-lubricated unison by classmates — and me!

Summers at SMC were an interesting mix: a summer camp for ten- to fourteen-year-olds, an athletic camp for high school students, and a training camp for the SF 49ers — who were notorious for such charming practices as defecating in the college pool.

After spending the summer between my freshman and sophomore years at my parents' new home in Anaheim, I decided not to repeat that mistake — and spent the next two summers at SMC as a camp counselor. The kids were fun, and the mix on campus was fascinating.

All the groups lived in the dorms; our kids and their counselors camped out once a week or so in a wooded part of the campus, a short walk from the dorms. We told ghost stories, toasted marshmallows, got insect bites, slept in sleeping bags, got dirty — all the traditional stuff. The kids loved it. These overnights had a kind of *McHale's Navy* feel to them.

One morning at the Anaheim house, during a visit from SMC, Ellen Ann and I stood chatting in the kitchen when I noticed a small paper cup sitting on the counter next to the sink. I looked over at it; it seemed to be filled with milk. "You're drinking milk, now?" I asked my mother as I picked the cup up for a sniff. The milk was heavily gin infused; it was early in the morning. Embarrassed at my discovery, Ellen Ann began to cry. "Is there anything you look forward to?" I asked her. "Grandchildren?" She merely shook her head and turned away.

At the college, we had a Jesuit theology professor who believed that the Vietnam War was unjust and immoral. A group of us went to Oakland one day to observe a protest he was involved in at the Oakland Induction Center. At one point, I crossed the street and joined both him and the protest — and my lifelong pacifism was born.

A group of us had signed up to take the LSAT, all of us headed to law school — or so we thought. The law profession had long been my assumed career destination. The morning of the exam, toward the end of our junior year, a couple of these guys came to my dorm room, and I was still in bed. Baffled, they asked what was going on. I replied that I had decided not to take the test (test taking was never that tough for me, so the test was not the issue) and not to go to law school. They moved on toward the goal we had all shared till then — and I went back to sleep, knowing that I now had to figure out a new path. Something had stirred in me, and I wasn't yet sure what. I have always been fairly good at following strong intuitions. Looking back, again, I'm struck that my parents were not involved in this decision; I don't recall them ever even opining on my career path or choices.

The night before graduation, we had a massive water fight in the dorm. The floors were wet and slippery — and so were all of us, most of us running around in our boxer shorts, throwing and dodging water at and from the others. It was great fun and the perfect way to close out our four years together. At some point, someone tried to tackle me, and I slipped and essentially did a face-plant, landing on my front teeth on the wet floor. A large chip broke off from one of them, which, when my mother noticed it after they arrived the next day, occasioned a rapid change of expression from "happy to see you; proud of you" to "what happened?"

All four of my grandparents attended the ceremony along with my parents; I've only fairly recently — as I've learned more about their early lives — realized how impactful that visit must have been for them. My mother said that Roy actually shed a few tears when I received my diploma. I was the only one of the five of us in our nuclear family to receive a degree.

My parents had driven up with the grandparents from Southern California in the 1960 Cadillac Roy had purchased a few years prior. The car developed some sort of difficulty and had to go in for repairs during their stay, just before the graduation ceremony. Michael loaned them his car. Albert joined us for dinner after the ceremony. Both acts were great honors.

None of my grandparents received any formal education beyond high school — and not all even graduated high school. Roy's parents were devout Catholics. I had the sense that the whole lot were impressed at their experience at SMC — both their grandson's college graduation and the attention they received from Brothers Albert and Michael. I suspect that they all went home with stories to tell.

A handful of my peers had very cool, newer-model cars during their time at the college. I did get my first car while there — my senior year — purchased for me by my parents: a nearly decade-old, dark-blue 1960 Chevy Biscayne. It wasn't flashy — and actually didn't last very long — but it was mine, and I was delighted to have it.

So I'd say that the Kings were nouveau middle class at that time, which I benefited from a great deal. I was also keenly aware that many of my classmates were of higher economic and social status than we were.

My years in the developing world just a few years after graduating SMC gave me my greatest life lesson on my privilege — and status — as an educated White American man — my sexual orientation and early trauma notwithstanding.

For me, leaving SMC was like being kicked out of the nest — a safe and protected place where I learned an enormous amount about myself and life — and some things from my various classes. The year that followed immediately after was in some ways an extension of my years at SMC.

Chapter Seven
High School
English Teacher

Four years after graduating from high school myself, while others proceeded on to law or other graduate studies, I became a high school teacher.

An older colleague asked me one day, clearly exasperated, if I considered the students to be my peers. I was twenty-one, my colleague in his midforties — slightly younger than my father; the oldest students were eighteen. I didn't see the students as my peers, but certainly felt greater generational and cultural affinity with the older students than with him. I don't recall how I responded to his question. There were several of us in our twenties on the faculty — all popular with the students.

The school, De La Salle High School (DLS), in Concord, California, belonged to the Christian Brothers; it was located not far at all from SMC. I started there as Mr. King, the new English teacher. I had no formal training in pedagogy or actual teaching.

My first day, the vice principal, a different Brother Michael — who sported a crew cut and was notorious for wearing white socks with his black robes — gave me a list of the classes I was teaching that fall, a set of keys, and pointed me toward my classroom. He wished me luck. That was my orientation to becoming a high school teacher.

I was assigned several sections of English and one of history. With the English classes, I at least had some passion and familiarity with the subject, so I stumbled along and did the best I could, learning as I went. The history class was an utter disaster since I had little content knowledge; I would read the textbook just ahead of the students' assignments. In my second semester, Brother Michael traded my history section for a PE section — only slightly better, since the students seemed to know what to do, and it was much less structured.

In retrospect, I'd give myself a D as a history teacher, a C minus as a PE instructor, and a B as an English teacher.

While I was criticized for my "rather loose classroom management" by a Christian Brother observer/evaluator, I was recognized at the same time for getting my students to write poetry and divide up into groups to create and design a novel — my creative attempts to impart an appreciation of literary form and genre.

I met my great life friend and brother from another mother, Nick (much more about him ahead), at DLS. He had been a "student brother" — Brother Geoffrey — at SMC when I was there, and knew of me, but our paths hadn't crossed that we recalled. He was three or so years older than I, and in his second year of teaching at DLS when I arrived. He taught Spanish, French, and drama; he enlisted me to assist in casting his plays, which I did with delight.

I lived in Berkeley during my year of teaching at DLS — a couple of blocks from People's Park, which exploded during my time there. For a few days, we had to show proof of residence to the National Guard troops who had secured the area, as only residents were allowed in.

Nick and I occasionally encountered our students on weekend evenings on Telegraph Avenue in Berkeley, and assumed that they — like us — were looking to score some weed. There was always a polite acknowledgment, and then we all continued on our way. No one seemed surprised to see the other there.

Older students occasionally crashed at my apartment, which I shared with three other recent SMC grads. It was Berkeley; it was the late '60s; it felt completely normal. Years later, two different DLS grads would become lovers of mine.

That spring, Nick; two seniors; Gail, a teacher friend from the Catholic girls' school across the street from DLS; and I drove to Baja California in my VW bus, where we camped on the beach for a few nights. This also seemed perfectly normal activity at the time.

On the way south, we stopped off for the night at my parents' home in Anaheim; Sharon was still living there. My father's lust for one of the students, Jimmy (one of the purest souls I have ever been blessed to know and with whom I had forged a bond unequaled in its depth to this day), was disgustingly palpable. I spent our brief visit essentially in full-protection mode — running interference, making sure that the two were never alone together, nor Jimmy within reach of the monster.

My father was aware of my efforts to outmaneuver him — and helpless to counter them — but I don't believe anyone else was any the wiser. We didn't stop at my parents' house on the return trip.

Also consistent with the times, boundaries were loose and obscured. One of the young teaching monks, who had been in the monastery with Nick and had been his lover there, was having an affair with the mother of one of the students. Another of the teaching monks maintained a communal household where he lived with several students — which felt odd and uncomfortable to me and others at the time (how had the parents allowed this?). His name was prominent on the list of clergy molesters from that time who were sued by those same students years later — as adults.

During this same time, a senior monk from SMC, in whom I had confided and come to know, asked me to accompany him to Carmel for a weekend, saying that he was undergoing a trying personal time and could use both a friend and a respite. He had been kind to me at the college, so, albeit a bit taken aback at the request, I agreed to accompany him.

When we checked in at the motel where he had reserved a room, noting right away that the room had only one bed and assuming this to have been a mistake, I went to the office and requested a rollaway bed for myself. It had not been a mistake. The monk's agenda all along had been that we "wind up in each other's arms," as he so charmingly put it. Despite being shocked and repulsed, I tried to accommodate his need, but failed miserably on all levels. I quickly ended my brief visit to his bed and returned to my own.

He had somehow managed to distort my confiding my early abuse to him into my wanting to have sex with him. What had been — for me — a treasured friendship dissolved in an instant into something quite foreign, infiltrated by lust and deception — unwelcome echoes of my relationship with my father, compounding and deepening my difficulties trusting older men.

The year after I graduated SMC, while in my first and only year at DLS, I filed papers with my draft board declaring myself a conscientious objector (CO) to all war, citing the teachings of Thomas Aquinas and pronouncements from Vatican Council II. At the time, this status had to be based on religious beliefs, and two years of approved "alternative service" had to be completed.

Nick also applied for CO status during this time. It was not an easy decision. Many of my contemporaries sought medical exemptions. Some fled to Canada. Some refused induction. My own decision followed a silent personal retreat at the Immaculate Heart Hermitage in Big Sur — where the resident hermits, adhering to medieval tradition, allowed persons to stay as their guests, providing them with a comfortable, if sparse, room/cell, a simple meal delivered three times a day, an invitation to participate or not in their religious services, and a requirement to participate in their vow of silence. As I meditated and contemplated my choices, I decided I could see no point in going to jail, did not want to flee the country, and taking a moral stand was most consistent with who I am.

An in-person interview with the draft board was required as part of the process. My interviewers were more interested in talking about SMC's football glory days than the substance of my application, and granted my request without objection — good, articulate White boy that I was. Roy was not amused. This was the first time that he disowned me.

Soon after I left the seminary and moved into a residence hall at SMC, my childhood friend Carlos (we met at a Catholic leadership conference in seventh grade, but lost touch after he went into the seminary after eighth grade) knocked on my dorm-room door one evening.

We remain very close friends today; I was his best man for his first wedding; he named his eldest son after me. In terms of Vietnam and the draft, because of his working-class Mexican background, Carlos felt that the CO route I had taken favored White boys and was much less available to those of his background, so on principle, he refused induction.

Carlos spent 1969–1971 in legal limbo, teaching middle school, starting a family, and waiting for his case to come up before a judge — while I spent the same period in the developing world as a teacher — as did Nick (which we'll see much more about below) — satisfying my alternative-service requirement.

My serenaded Big Sur tryst with Lisa occurred the summer after my year of teaching at DLS, and before departing for Laos.

Chapter Eight
Around the World

Laos

In my last glimpse of them for the next two years, out the side airplane window, Sharon had her head down, her forehead resting on her arm; our parents stood next to her, looking distractedly somber. Four years of college and my year of teaching at DLS had revealed intoxicating worlds beyond my toxic family; I was determined to only go forward from there.

When I received my assignment, we had all needed to look Laos up in the atlas; none of us could say exactly where it was.

Our first stop was Washington, DC, for orientation with International Voluntary Services (IVS) — the NGO I had chosen and that had been approved by my draft board to satisfy my civilian-service requirement as a CO — as a teacher for the next two years. It was August 1969. Nick had also accepted assignment with IVS, in satisfaction of his CO alternative-service requirement, to a teaching post in Algeria — where, unbeknownst to either of us at the time, I would join him the following year.

In DC, we were advised that two volunteers had been killed in an ambush by the Pathet Lao (the Vietnam War was still in full force) the prior week. We were all given the option not to move forward with our assignments. We all moved forward.

The next flight was DC to Anchorage, then an overnight in Tokyo before continuing on to Hong Kong and our eventual short flight to Vientiane, Laos, in a vintage DC-3, which we boarded while its tail was sitting on the runway. Some of its passengers held live chickens in their laps, and all of them eyed us young Americans with wide-eyed curiosity. We were, I'm sure, no less wide-eyed.

Laos, as a country, was created by the Geneva Accords of 1954; its three historic kingdoms — North, Middle, and South — had been unified in 1946. Three of us volunteers — all COs — were assigned as directors of Lao American Cultural Centers — one to Luang Prabang in the North, which served as the royal capital after the unification, one to Savannakhet in the Center, and me to Pakse in the South.

Landlocked, the Mekong River forms the small country's western boundary. It borders Thailand, Vietnam, Cambodia, and what today is Myanmar. The Viet Kong worked closely with the Pathet Lao in its war against first the French, and then the Americans and the South Vietnamese. The Ho Chi Minh Trail ran from North Vietnam, through Laos and Cambodia, as a military supply route for the North.

Pakse was the capital of the Kingdom of Champassak prior to the unification of the three kingdoms; even today, its population is less than 100,000. Our small contingent of Americans stationed there gathered once a week at the airport to collect our mail, which was flown in from the capital, Vientiane. We were CIA families, USAID personnel, US military attachés, and a few volunteer English teachers, mostly

American, one British — my roommate — blond, tall, sweet Steve — big crush — unrequited. We of course all got to know one another, which would never have happened in other circumstances.

A major delight in living and working in a different country is that different norms apply — and one has to figure them out while setting aside one's own.

We had been advised by veteran volunteers at orientation in Vientiane that one could obtain weed in the local markets, but needed to ask for "tea" in order to do so. Sure enough, barely settled in Pakse, we visited the local market and found the tea section, where a vendor smiled broadly when she saw us and gestured us over to her wares.

Many folks chewed betel nut — a mild intoxicant — much of the day, turning their gums a bright red. These were very laid-back folks.

In Laos, for example, two soldiers — or policemen — holding hands nonchalantly while walking down the street, their weapons slung over their free shoulders, was a common sight. Likewise, schoolboys lounged in leisure, draped partially over one another. Young monks in the temples lay about on hot afternoons, in saffron robes, bodies intersecting in the shade. None of these examples carried the slightest erotic/ sexual connotation — though all would have been seen in that light at home.

In a social setting, one was expected to sit such that their head was lower than that of the person present with the highest social status — and — it was rude to sit with one ankle resting on the opposite knee such that the bottom of one's foot was pointing at another person.

I also learned that, while the modern world had somewhat reached Lao cities, the lived reality in the more distant mountain villages had likely not changed significantly for centuries. A local pilot invited a couple of us to come along one day in his small plane for a visit to such a village about an hour's flight from Pakse. After we deplaned and were walking down the main path into the village proper, we were approached by some villagers who beseeched us to join what turned out to be the majority of the local population who were assembled under a traditional Lao house — on stilts.

We agreed, curious about the urgency. The people gathered there were drinking rice wine from long reeds that all reached into a single large vessel. It was explained to us that the house belonged to an elderly woman who was very ill. The village gathered to lend spirit to the woman's own failing spirit; the wine was an instrument of communion and connectivity, perhaps doing its part in freeing individual spirits and assisting them to join the collective. We were greeted as exotic foreigners who had come from the sky at just this crucial moment — whose spirits were bound to be powerful, a gift from the heavens to bolster the woman's flagging spirit.

We of course joined the others and took our turns at the reeds as they passed from mouth to mouth. I have no idea whether the woman's health improved, but was struck and impressed to this day at the powerful belief that we collectively possess powers of spirit that can heal one another.

It didn't take long for us three COs to discover that our Lao American Cultural Associations were essentially English-language schools to impart sufficient English to the local populations that they could then work with the Americans in support of the war effort.

Before long, we independently requested a meeting at the IVS in-country headquarters in the capital, Vientiane, to impart a singular message: neither we nor IVS belonged in these roles. IVS was under contract with USAID for our positions, which added a layer of complexity.

IVS agreed to cancel the contract and asked that we all serve out the year; we would then be given a choice of second-year assignments, either in-country or elsewhere where IVS had available postings. I asked to be posted to Algeria, which I had done initially, but my French was weak then, and volunteers there taught English in French to local students. Nick worked from within Algeria to get me assigned to the same town. We succeeded.

But the year in Laos was an unimaginably rich and indelibly impactful one.

Steve and I at first inhabited a wooden house on stilts, a bit north of the town center, not far from the local USAID offices and the airport. There was a Vietnamese Buddhist temple across the dirt road from our house (Pakse's population at the time was primarily Lao, Vietnamese, and Indian — with some Thai and Cambodian); it flew colorful flags and pennants when they hosted festivals.

I remember our house having two bedrooms — a simple wall of raw-wood planks between them — a shower and a substantial front porch, large enough for five or six to gather outside on warm days and evenings. There must have also been a kitchen, but I can't picture it.

Memories of the porch include a monkey standing on my shoulders and searching through my hair, and one hot afternoon when a group of us were sitting, chatting, and enjoying a beer when a man from the nearby mountains came around trying to sell his wares — crude carvings and odds and ends. No one wanted to buy anything, but I offered him a beer — which he delightedly accepted — and in turn placed a simple brass bracelet around my left wrist, one strand of brass — which I wore for many years until it broke in two one day. I still have the pieces. I learned and observed during my time in SE Asia that many wore brass or gold bracelets — believed to bring good fortune. They varied in size and sophistication, in correlation with one's class and riches; the grandest had elegant and elaborate carvings. I liked my simple one.

There were two low-precision Pathet Lao rocket attacks during the time we lived in that house — most likely aimed at the nearby USAID offices. During the first one, in the very early morning, debris fell on the metal roof of our simple domicile. A team was sent afterwards to dig a foxhole under the stilts, so we'd have someplace to go if there were more shellings.

As soon as we heard the now-familiar whistling of approaching rockets, signaling the second attack, we raced to our foxhole, where we remained until the attack ended. As frightening as they were, I don't recall there being significant damage from either attack, but we did learn that the USAID offices were hit and that a glass-framed portrait of then POTUS Richard Nixon had been knocked from the wall, glass shattered.

After the second attack, IVS decided to move us into town and away from the targets to the north. Our household expanded to include a local student, Soupho, whose family could not afford to feed and lodge him as he attended the local secondary school, so he moved in with us. He was our trusty translator. Roy, a somewhat-older American volunteer, eerily with the same name as my father, and, I think, another American volunteer also joined Steve and me there.

Roy and Steve taught at the local lycée — French-system secondary school. Steve also taught some classes for me — ours was an evening school; we used the classrooms that the lycée used during the day. We were open to the general population, and our students were of different ages.

The house was a two-story, cement, French-style building with a traditional Lao communal bathing trough in back. While our wages were pitiful by American standards ($200 per month, as I recall), there we made enough to travel in the region, when we had free time, and to hire a lovely local woman to shop and cook for us.

It wasn't long before we all noticed that Roy would summon some of his male students — one at a time — for a personalized review of their schoolwork...in his bedroom...with the door closed. Soupho was the one who sounded the alarm, as the students, horrified, began to confide in him that Roy was sodomizing them in his room, how painful it was, and that they were threatened with dire consequences if they told anyone.

It fell to me to confront Roy and tell him that this behavior had to stop immediately and that any further occurrence would result in his being expelled from the house...and IVS being notified.

Looking back, I'm not sure why I gave him even that much consideration. Perhaps some kind of learned helplessness after my experience with my father? My first impulse was to protect the students, BUT Roy was raping his students in our home! I should have had him arrested.

My recollection is that he was angrier at being confronted than embarrassed or ashamed. I was furious, knowing all too well the insidious effects of Roy's molestation of these young students. I doubt that we stopped Roy altogether from his predatory behavior, but likely drove it more underground.

One evening after class, I was approached by a local, saffron-robed Buddhist monk. In simple but understandable English, he explained that the monks were not allowed to attend classes with women — our classes were all mixed — and asked if I would be willing to teach a separate class for him and his fellow monks at the temple in the center of town. My days were free, I liked this gentle man, and I was intrigued by the monks I saw frequently as I traveled throughout the area. So — in spite of warnings from government-affiliated Americans that the monks were "leeches" and possible Pathet Lao spies — I agreed to teach the class — which turned out to be one of the high points of my year in Laos.

In one class, there were twenty to twenty-five monks of varying ages and proficiency in English. As we became more and more comfortable with one another, a young monk asked me who Jesus was. I replied that Jesus was to Christians as Buddha was to Buddhists. I was met with quite a loud chorus of protest: there was only one Buddha, and he had no equal. I replied that many Christians would say the same about Jesus.

Later, visiting the monks in their residence, I asked if they could teach me about Buddha. After exchanging some puzzled looks, one said simply, "Be with us."

Some mornings, I got up very early — before they started school and before it got too hot — to play tennis with Soupho and two of his friends. We'd sit afterwards at a corner café for a lemonade before heading off in different directions to begin our day. Often, our lemonade moment coincided with the procession of a line of monks I knew walking solemnly down the road, begging bowls in hand. By tradition, they were fed by the community, to whose service they had dedicated their lives. I always tried to make them laugh as they passed by, and often succeeded, to my and their great delight...though they chided me privately afterwards for compromising their solemnity. This behavior — and the fact that I affectionately called my saffron friends monkeys — was scandalous in the eyes of Soupho and his friends.

I had been issued a USAID Jeep in my role as director — so I was pretty conspicuous. I was all of twenty-two when I arrived in Laos, and was taken aback when soldiers and police saluted me when I drove through town, especially since I naïvely considered myself wholly separate from the war effort.

Pakse was the central and largest village in a more-or-less concentric clustering of villages, which, taken together, formed the city. As I got to know the monks, my class grew, and monks came from the surrounding villages as well as from the center of Pakse. So I circled around the various villages, collected as many monks as I could fit in my open-sided Jeep, and took them to class — saffron robes flying and the mostly quiet young monks squealing with glee as we drove through town. It was quite the sight — one which had not been seen before.

Toward the end of my year in Laos, the monk who had initially asked me to hold the class for him and his fellow monks invited me to travel with him to his home village to meet his family and, nearby, an elderly monk who had been his teacher. I knew that this invitation — while on one level an indication of friendship — was also a profound honor.

One of the local CIA families and I became acquainted. Their son Mike had been expelled from his Swiss boarding school and sent to live with his parents in Pakse. A rare, available native-English speaker, I offered some rudimentary coaching and put him to work teaching at my school. He was a hit with the students, and enjoyed himself. His parents were relieved.

Mike's father and I became unlikely friends — wherein we acknowledged one another's differences in values and worldviews. He showed me with pride his personal weapon — the Colt .45 he had been given by his father — and invited me to visit his secret — and technically nonexistent — base on the Ho Chi Minh Trail, where he trained and oversaw a small army of Hmong tribesmen — on the condition that I take no photos and never write about it in such a way that he or it could be identified. He seemed intrigued and genuinely respectful of the fact that I was a pacifist, did not own a gun, and was opposed to all war.

I did visit his base; it was utterly fascinating.

Luang Prabang was the royal capital and an absolute visual delight with its ornately gilded temples and related structures. On my one visit there, with another volunteer, we stopped by a local opium den. I had been curious about opium since arriving in Laos, but also cautious, as I feared that I might like it quite a lot. I did. One reclined on a bamboo mat, next to a wizened older man who filled his long brass pipe with opium, lit it, and placed the far end into one's waiting mouth. Eventually, one was rolled over next to the other bodies on the mat to enjoy the effects — which were quite decidedly out-of-body. Unfortunately, we had a plane to catch back to Pakse, so had to get up and function well before we might have chosen to otherwise. Nausea and overall imbalance quickly took over from the floating euphoria of lying on the mat. The flight home was not pleasant.

Nick meanwhile had settled into his first year of teaching in Algeria. We wrote letters back and forth fairly frequently. We had both been closeted during our time at DLS, but worked up the courage to come out to one another in our correspondence. We decided to use the word *onions* as code for sex. I have no idea why, but we obviously felt that this was a taboo topic. We were never lovers.

For the 1969 Christmas holidays, a volunteer friend, Fred, and I traveled to Cambodia, where we visited the capital, Phnom Penh, and stayed in Krong Siem Reap, from which we bicycled through the astonishing eleventh- and twelfth-century temples at Angkor Wat, then only recently partially uncovered after decades of having been consumed by jungle.

We took in a movie while in Cambodia — which was preceded in the theater by a newsreel of current events, focusing on the war going on around us at the time. In one scene, a US fighter jet was shot out of the sky — at which the audience cheered boisterously, loud and long. It was a great — and frankly, in the moment, stunning — lesson in perspective. We were definitely not in Kansas anymore.

Also in Cambodia, we met two charming and delightful British girls, Maggie and Suan Po, who joined us in some of our travels…and whom Nick and I visited in England the following summer.

It was routine for us to check with local military authorities before heading out in any direction by road. One day, we had planned a picnic for a group of students at a favorite swimming spot north of Pakse, and dutifully checked in ahead of time. We were advised that, due to guerrilla activity in that area, we could not travel north that day. So we headed south instead, where no issues had been reported.

In spring of 1970, the US invaded Cambodia, which constituted a significant escalation of the war effort is SE Asia. The tranquil, carefree country Fred and I had experienced over the holidays was suddenly no more. One evening, after I learned of the invasion, I could not contain my anger during my classes. It clearly made the students uncomfortable to hear my comments…and they asked to return to the lesson.

Soon after, on another evening after classes and after my outburst, a man I didn't know approached me outside my school and told me, "They know your Jeep — you can travel freely." Both chilling and in some odd way comforting, this message brought into sharp relief that the Pathet Lao were integrated with the local population and did not wear uniforms or move in groups — at least in the daylight.

I was also informed by students after this mysterious visit that I had been assumed to be CIA before I spoke out in my classes against the US war effort.

A local woman very much wanted to have my baby; I did not share that interest. My year in Laos was a painfully — and privately confusedly — celibate one. But it was hardly without riches of many kinds.

While I was deeply conflicted during my year in Laos — contemplating suicide and struggling alone amidst bouts of deep depression, against what I then considered the "cancer of my homosexuality" — I was able to protect the innocence of several young men against a predator named Roy. And I was warmly embraced by a people who were loving, kind, compassionate, and generous. Both were deeply healing — in ways I didn't fully understand then that I sorely needed.

As word spread of my impending departure from Laos, two remarkable things happened.

One, a favorite student and friend of Soupho's, Somdit, gave me a small Buddha carved from animal bone, to protect me in my travels. Somdit took me to meet a friend or relation of his, who crafted a gold border in which to encase the Buddha, while keeping it visible from front and back, and a handmade gold chain to then be able to wear it around my neck. I still wear — and treasure — this gift today.

Two, dozens gathered for a traditional Baci ceremony with singing and food and celebrants (students and their families, mostly) one-by-one tying a simple piece of string around my wrist, each then rubbing the knot to impart their good wishes. By the end, I had a wrist full of good wishes, which I wore for weeks during my journey from Laos to Algeria.

Coming Out in Algeria

If Laos whispered its sexuality as a society, Algeria roared its own in comparison. I was asked — by students in class — whether or not I was circumcised, and if I would come to teach one day in my underwear.

On a weekend visit to his village in the Atlas Mountains, during which we shared a bed in his family's home, a student attempted to sodomize me. Another student waited for me one day outside of class and asked if we could kiss. One student — after we had come to know one another — confided that he had fucked several of the family's animals.

The generation of my students' fathers — and many, in fact, of their own fathers — had vanquished the French in a long and bitter war of independence — at a very high cost — so it was not surprising that my students held the French, in general, in contempt. The sexualized expression of this contempt on the part of my students was to proclaim with haughty disdain that the French had small uncircumcised penises — whereas the Algerians had much larger, circumcised ones.

But before I dive more deeply into my year in Algeria, the time and journey between Laos and there is too consequential not to be described.

As a condition of my transfer to Algeria, IVS arranged for me to study French — in Nice, at a music school nestled in the hills just outside the city center. It was extremely tough duty, but I vowed to give it my best shot. Preparing for my journey to France, I sat in a travel agency in Vientiane, where there was a map of the world on the wall behind the person helping me. We could look at all of what lay between Laos and Paris, where I was to meet Nick.

The agent explained to me that my ticket allowed for as many stopovers as I wanted. I had essentially no money, so we set to work selecting flights with meals…and I was able to stop off in Malaysia, Singapore, Nepal, India, Afghanistan, Iran, Turkey, and Greece — where I met up with some California friends, including the SMC classmate who had serenaded Lisa and me during our tryst in Big Sur.

So I experienced some very hot curry and delighted in the tropical waters in Malaysia, marveled at the clean streets in Singapore, was frustrated by the fog in my hopes of seeing Mt. Everest in Nepal, wandered languidly through the Taj Mahal in India, got stoned with a previously-unknown fellow traveler in Afghanistan — and explored the dusty neighborhoods of Kabul together — spent hours on foot getting lost and finding my way again in Tehran, got thrown out of the Grand Mosque in Istanbul for lying on the floor to better see the ceiling, and had deeply healing days and nights in Greece with friends…with lots of ouzo, retsina, swims at all times of day and night in the ubiquitous Mediterranean, and joyful laughter — all before my eventual flight to Paris.

Nick's smiling face greeted me at Charles de Gaulle Airport in Paris; he and it were a delight to see.

Not long after our joyful reunion in Paris, Nick and I crossed the Channel and visited Maggie and Suan Po in London. Later, Nick drove me to Nice, in a recently purchased — with his roommate from Algeria, Georges — Peugeot 403. During my time "studying" in Nice, Nick would come and go — to Italy to visit distant relatives in his mother's ancestral village, and on various explorations around the area.

He was also in Nice a fair amount of the time, and he, Margrethe (a young Danish fledgling journalist who was working on a master's thesis — with comparable seriousness to my study of French), and I became a threesome of joy — laughing, drinking wine, cavorting on the beaches and in cafes all around the area. We all became lifelong friends, Nick gone now and Margrethe and I like brother and sister over fifty years later. We three were last together in Paris in 1996, our mutual delight and uproarious laughter alive and well over the years.

One wonderful memory from that time is of Margrethe — perhaps a bit tipsy — holding a pair of my boxer shorts (she had never encountered such a thing, and found them hilarious — we were never lovers) out of the Peugeot's passenger-side front window, like a flag or banner, as we drove gaily down the Promenade des Anglais.

Nick and I spent Christmas 1970 with Margrethe and her family in Copenhagen; Margrethe later visited Nick and me in Algeria.

Another fond memory from that remarkable summer in Nice was of receiving a telegram from Carlos, announcing the birth of his first child, whom he and Sally named Patrick Neal. I was deeply honored — and Patrick and I have been in each other's lives from that moment forward. Patrick is in his fifties now.

And I would be remiss in not mentioning Gottfried, who was also at the music school in Nice — whether teaching or studying, I don't recall. He was tall and stately, a warm, fun, and funny man, a bit older than the others of us who played so joyfully together that summer. He taught at a gymnasium in his native Stuttgart and was a passionate avocational opera singer. He joined Margrethe in visiting Nick and me in Tizi Ouzou the following spring, and the four of us ventured together into the Sahara. Nick and I would in turn visit him in Stuttgart that summer.

It was also in Nice that I received my first blow job — from a very-comfortable-in-his-gay-identity American music professor who was teaching at the school for the summer. In some ways, that act set the stage for a very sexually alive, explicit, and life-changing year in Algeria — a kind of bridge between that and my celibate, shame-filled, lonely, and frustrated/confused year in Laos...and an unforeseen foundation for the post-Stonewall gay reality that I encountered — with delight — upon my return to the USA.

But...lots happened before that.

Armed with my only slightly improved command of the French language — the language of instruction and social intercourse in Algeria for Westerners — Nick and I began our leisurely drive to North Africa, leaving Nice and our delightful summer there behind. The new academic year beckoned, and it was time to get back to work, eventually.

In Burgos, Spain, after having visited the magnificent cathedral there, Nick for some reason affectionately dubbed me "the Irish pornographer." I wish I remembered the context. I've never — before or since — produced or participated in pornography. At the same time, I have no objection to it as long as it's nonexploitative and involves only consenting adults — and admit to being a consumer myself.

But — there in Burgos — we both knew why he called me that. It had to do with my hypersexualized way of seeing and relating to the world — something which I understand today as an abuse survivor, but then just thought was life. I do recall wearing an Irish-style casquette at the time — so that was likely also a factor.

I also remember, from that drive, a night spent in the car in a Madrid residential neighborhood and seeking Don Quixote and Sancho Panza's La Mancha as we continued south — not realizing that La Mancha was a several-province region of Spain rather than a particular, albeit mythical, village — and finding only a statue of the two legendary companions and idealists — in front of a gas station — in otherwise-naked countryside. Not even a windmill!

In Rabat, Morocco, we were offered the services of one young man's sister — and then brother. We politely declined. As we entered Algeria, we marveled at the largely untouched and no-less-magnificent-than-those-on-the-European-side-of-the-same-Mediterranean beaches, mile after mile.

Finally reaching Algiers, I experienced my second IVS in-country orientation — and met fellow volunteers who would soon be scattered around the country. One was a friend and fellow SMC graduate — complete surprise, I had no idea — and others who became friends for many years to come.

After orientation, Nick and I proceeded east to Tizi Ouzou, the capital of the Berber region, Kabylie — its ancient villages nestled in the Atlas Mountains. Nick had spent the prior year there, so already knew his way around. Kabylie had been the center of some of the fiercest fighting of the then recent — and aforementioned — war of independence from France (1954–1962). The Berbers are the indigenous, non-Arabic inhabitants of North Africa — often nomadic. In Kabylie, they are mountain dwellers.

Nick returned to the teachers' training school where he had taught the prior year. I was assigned to Lycée Amirouche, a newly opened — and the sole — secondary school for a region roughly the size of California. The French had severely limited access to education during their colonization of Algeria. The sons — and a very few daughters — of the war dead were given priority for enrollment. I was the only American on the faculty; my colleagues came from France, Russia, Syria, Egypt, Canada…and other countries I cannot recall at the moment. We were quite the mix.

I was twenty-three when I reported for duty in the fall of 1970. French was the language of instruction; mine was still rudimentary.

The students were overwhelmingly male. In one of my classes, there were three girls who were the best students of them all. The trio sat together and ignored the boys' taunts; they outshone and outclassed the boys handily. In my other classes, there were no girls.

At the end of each term, all instructors met to discuss and evaluate the students and decide who would and would not advance to the next grade. The three girls were in the rough equivalent of ninth grade and up for promotion to the more advanced classes and final years of secondary study.

As each instructor spoke at the meeting, it became clear that none of them intended to advance the girls — any of them. When my turn came, I simply stated that they were all excellent students and that I would definitely vote to advance all of them. Palpable scorn consumed my colleagues' faces; there was clearly an unwritten code that allowed only so many girls to study, and an assumption that none would advance to the higher levels. Of course, no one told me that — and it would not have mattered.

Later, after that meeting, I was called into the office of the gentleman in charge of faculty and academics. He advised me, harshly, *"Vous êtes insolent"* (you are insolent). I was proud of myself — when later relating the incident to Nick — that I had the presence of mind to summon the proper French in the moment to respond, *"Je ne suis pas obligé a supporter ça"* (essentially, I'm not obliged to put up with that)... and walk out of his office. We did not become great friends.

Four of us — Nick, Georges, Jean-Claude, and I — shared a French-style villa in town. I was the only one of us who taught at the lycée, the other three at the same teachers' training school. There was one bathroom and a shared kitchen. Nick and I had adjoining rooms at one end of the house, while Jean-Claude and Georges had rooms at the other. We prepared and consumed meals — and copious amounts of Algerian wine — separately and together, and often with friends and colleagues.

Our schools observed a long midday break, as was the French custom. Like our fellows, we would stop for a freshly-baked baguette on the way back to the house, where we'd enjoy a leisurely lunch. Returning to teach the afternoon classes was always difficult — particularly when we succumbed to the temptation of a glass of wine with our midday meal.

A German shepherd showed up in our front garden, a length of thick wire tight around her neck. Initially, she was snarling and afraid, but also hungry — for food *and* affection.

We tossed food at her, which she accepted eagerly while keeping her distance and us under a constant watchful gaze. Little by little, she started to trust us. She let us take the wire off. She let us pet her. She eventually came into the house and became our pet. We called her Crotch — intentionally provocative — so we could enjoy hearing our students, roommates, and non-English speaking local friends call her without knowing her name's meaning.

Some students paused to chat while passing by the house; others came into the yard on warm days and pet the dog. One young student stopped by, only to flee when he saw and heard that there were women friends in the house. We got to know some of our visitors better than others, and those often spent time inside with us. A few of the older, twenty-something students occasionally stayed overnight, and some shared our beds (Nick's and mine — as far as I recall, not Georges's or Jean-Claude's).

Sean, a Canadian teacher also living in Tizi Ouzou, kindly loaned me his VW bus one day to give a student a ride home to Algiers, the capital — where his family had summoned him with some urgency. Driving — perhaps a bit too fast — along the open highway, we were pulled over by a burly police officer, his motorcycle lights flashing insistently. He approached our vehicle and, assuming I was French, began to angrily berate me, asking if I thought that the speed limit did not apply to me, implying that I thought myself superior.

My student, Rezki, leaned over and said to the officer in Arabic, "He's American."

Instantly, the officer's indignant scowl was replaced with a wide smile, and his eyes lit up. "American!" he proclaimed. "Are you enjoying your stay? Do you like our country?" We chatted amiably for a few more moments before he wished us well and went on his way.

Such was — at that time — the sharp contrast in how we Americans, versus the despised French, were viewed by the Algerians.

Three students from Nick's school — friends Said and Belkacem, and Rabah (who was at the time also in a relationship with Marc, a married French teacher there) — became local friends with benefits (none exclusive). For me, they, in aggregate, were my first adult experience with sex that was warm, natural, relaxed, fun, spontaneous, mutual. They changed me in ways that I needed to experience. He who had left California guilt-ridden, confused, and painfully conflicted about his sexual orientation saw the window of gradual acceptance begin to open in Nice, and continue to do so during his time in Algeria.

Also important was working things out clearly with Beatrice, one of our great friends in Tizi Ouzou — she and her husband were frequent social companions — my lack of attraction sexually to her. While I was very fond of her and other women in my life, there was simply — I came finally to recognize and admit — no sexual attraction.

This same young gentleman, however, at the same time, had little awareness of the relationship between his childhood sexual abuse and his current relational life — sexual and otherwise. This all surfaced and became a major focus later — after returning to the States.

Years later, as mentioned above, I wrote professionally about the intersection of childhood sexual abuse and sexual orientation — drawing upon both my own experience and that of several of my clients in my clinical practice. Working out my true sexual orientation was the easy part, compared with the depth and complexities of working out the residue and impact of childhood abuse on my relational life — a several years' undertaking — ongoing.

Ironically, overt homosexuality was not accepted in Algeria, but — since the sexes were separated until marriage — same-sex sex play (at least for the males, absent penetration) was highly stigmatized but tacitly OK as long as not publicly acknowledged, nor overtly romantic. Males who were known to receive sexually were seen as having assumed the female role, were stigmatized for life, and could not escape or change to the more masculine posture. It was OK to assume the active role — no stigma whatsoever.

On one of my many visits to students' villages — which would often include a visit to the grave of the father, who had been killed in the recent war — I was approached by a charming and attractive young man who was shooed away by my host. It was later explained that he was passive with men, and I did not want to be seen associating with him, his evident charms notwithstanding.

Penetration was therefore simply not a part of my Algerian lovers' and my sexual interactions — minus that one attempt by an overzealous student when I was visiting his village with him.

Rabah joined Nick and me one evening at a favorite restaurant in town, which I recall being called the Baghdad. We encountered colleagues there; two we dubbed — behind their backs — the "silly Syrians" because they were Syrian and seemed to laugh and giggle a lot. We came to know the staff well. The evening that Rabah was with us, when our by-then-familiar waiter set my plate down in front me, there was a solitary French fry standing straight up in my couscous. The three of us — and the waiter — laughed heartily at this recognition of what Rabah's presence at the table implied.

On another of my visits to a student's village, I was honored to have been sufficiently trusted and accepted to be included in a healing ceremony one evening. The women were behind a curtain, separate from the men, where they keened in varying volumes throughout as people on both sides of the curtain played drums and tambourine-like instruments in a hypnotic, repetitive fashion. The priestlike figure circulated amongst the men with a pipe, which he offered to whoever gestured toward him. I gestured and he offered; I think it was hashish. At various points in the ceremony, someone shot up from their seated position, danced feverishly, and then dropped to the floor. My student explained later that villagers believed this ceremony — in summoning the collective energies of those present (very reminiscent of the mountain-village experience in Laos) — could heal anything from infertility to fever to chronic illness.

That spring, Tim, a DLS graduate who had been traveling in Europe, came to visit. He was a lovely soul whom both Nick and I were delighted to see. We enjoyed sharing our

Algeria world with him. He came to one of my classes and shared aspects of his life in California with my students. They asked about his family and their home. He responded in part by creating on the board a rough diagram of his family home. The students were amazed at the number of rooms it had.

At some point, Georges returned to France and took the Peugeot with him. So Nick and I purchased another in-country — an older '50s black tank of an automobile, one similar to those driven by many of the few Algerians who owned cars.

When Margrethe and Gottfried visited in the spring, Margrethe quickly learned that long dresses and modest dress were in order, as catcalls and ugly stares welcomed her when she first arrived attired in her typical Scandinavian fashion. Gottfried's booming tenor bounced off the walls of the house during their visit and filled it with wondrous new sound.

We four took the new-old Peugeot south — to the northern edges of the Sahara. We visited Biskra, where André Gide lived and wrote for many years, as well as Bou Saâda, 1,000-year-old Ghardaïa, Laghouat, and the ancient Berber-founded city of Ouargla — our southernmost stop.

At one point, the old Peugeot overheated, and we had to stop in the desert and let it recover until we could coax it to start up again. There were no people or buildings in sight in any direction. Sand drifted across the road. I climbed a nearby dune and wrote names and other miscellany in the sand; everything disappeared within minutes, the sand in constant motion. We were all quite relieved when the car started up again, and we could resume our journey.

At another, we had to wait while a lone gentleman drove a herd of a hundred or so camels across the road in front of us. He stopped and asked if we had any cigarettes, which we did not.

One indelible memory of this trip: Nick and Gottfried shared a room in the hotel where we stopped late one night, and Margrethe and I shared another. Young, blonde Margrethe proved irresistible to some men who tried to break into the room during the night, as we were sleeping, yelling for her to come out. Margrethe and I barricaded the door with all the furniture we could move, and I threw loose objects — including bottles filled with water — at the door each time another attempt was made to enter despite my yelling — with my limited and imperfect French profanities — for them to go away. In the end, they did go away; we did not sleep another wink that night.

In the morning, Nick and Gottfried were shocked to hear our story, as they both had slept soundly and did not hear a thing! The hotel receptionist was suspiciously charming and professional when we went to check out.

The year passed quickly, as the one before had in Laos, and the goodbyes were equally painful — attachments, again, of surprising depth developed over such a brief period of time in yet another heretofore wholly foreign land and culture. There was no Baci ceremony, as there had been in Laos — instead, several long farewell visits to the house, a farewell feast with colleagues who had become friends, and several groups or pairings of students — and local lovers — who came and spent some time before we parted ways.

We sold our Peugeot to members of Said's family, an hours-long process that involved spirited bargaining and an obligatory feast in their village home.

Beyond Algeria — Homeward Bound

Summer 1971 found Nick and me again adventuring in Europe. We purchased a 750cc Triumph motorcycle with sidecar in London and traversed parts of England, Belgium, France, Holland, and Germany. Before leaving England, we visited Steve, my roommate from Laos, at his home in Ashford, Surrey. After crossing the Channel, we made our way to Stuttgart and visited dear Gottfried, and met his family and students. It was an absolute delight to see both of these lovely souls in their home territory. We also got to visit Jean-Claude (home for a summer visit from Algeria; he would return in the fall) in Metz, to reunite with fellow-American IVS volunteers from Algeria, Warren and Susie, in Paris, and from there to Nemours, where we visited with Georges and his family.

We were taken aback, entering one French village, that people stopped and stared. It was explained to us that the Nazis had used motorcycles with sidecars — with machine guns mounted on them — during WWII — and that seeing us enter their village all those years later was chilling and evoked painful memories.

In time, Nick and I began to wear on one another — having spent so very much time together — and he prepared to return to the States, leaving me with the motorcycle and arranging its shipment back to the States.

Fortuitously, Sharon arrived in Paris at about the same time. Our notoriously tight father had financed her trip to get her away from a boyfriend of whom he did not approve. Our reunion was pure joy! After two years, we had so much to discuss and learn about the other's life. We were blessed with the opportunity to cement our always-present love and connection at a new level of development for us both. She was nineteen, and I was twenty-two when we had last met; now she was twenty-one, and I was twenty-four. There were stories to tell!

We traveled together in France and England for a couple of weeks, before depositing the bike in Le Havre for shipment to Boston. One morning, as we emerged from our tent, a French couple nearby held up their new infant and asked if we two were ready to make some of our own. Once they learned that we were siblings, the topic of conversation changed.

Earlier, traveling with Georges, we had the good fortune of having a mechanical breakdown — in France, in August — when the whole country goes on vacation. The good fortune part was that — after Georges spent hours calling and calling to find a mechanic who would fix the bike — a lovely couple took pity on us in Villefranche-sur-Saône; they and their close circle of biker folk essentially adopted us for several days as we waited for parts to be delivered and needed repairs to be made. They toured us around their part of the world, wined and dined us with their scrumptious Beaujolais wines, and housed us; they could not have been more generous with their time and hospitality.

Sharon and I concluded our time together in Paris — a city we both adored and felt very much at home therein. We flew into Boston and stayed some days with the Macklins, our mother's parents, at their very familiar home in Clinton. Mac and Jeanne lived in an apartment upstairs, the grandparents in the house below. They were, as always, warm and gracious, generous and uncomplicated.

My grandmother was a fabulous cook; people who were lucky enough to experience them still rave today about her pies. My grandfather, sadly, died less than three years after Sharon and I visited — at age seventy-three from emphysema contracted during his long years of working in factories. I don't recall there having been any sign at the time of our visit that he was ill; this long and rich visit was our last with this good and loving man. Our grandmother was bereft without him. She lived for several more years, but shrank into a state of fearful and paranoid delusion — spending her last years living with Mac and Jeanne on the Cape, before her own death in a nearby nursing home, at eighty-nine.

The idea in stopping off in Boston was that we would pick up the motorcycle and drive it to California. BUT it took forever to arrive, and we both — first Sharon, after about a week, and then me, after nearly a month — headed west on our own. Fortunately, Warren was nearby and offered to take delivery of the bike when it finally arrived.

So I bid farewell to the Macklins and boarded a Greyhound for the trip west — which turned out to be the perfect conveyance — slow and easy, a chance to absorb the contemporary sights and sounds of the country I had left two years prior, but which of course had continued to evolve without me.

My two years as a volunteer teacher in the developing world were over. I was back in the good old USA. Now what? I had only the vaguest of plans.

Chapter Nine
Vagabond Years/Essential Wanderings

Phase 1: Northern California

Giant pornographic images flooded the walls above and behind the bar, thunderously, somehow louder than the accompanying disco music whose repetitive bass rhythmically shook the building. San Francisco seemed the natural location to try and pick up where I had left off, but this was a new and different San Francisco to me. Post-Stonewall, pre-AIDS gay liberation had arrived, and what had previously been known only in shadow now cavorted proudly in the brightest light of day. It was a bit overwhelming, and I was quite unsure how to navigate it all. The year was 1971, and I was back.

The Stonewall Riots took place in NYC in June of 1969, and Woodstock in August of the same year — Stonewall at the same time that I was preparing to leave for Laos, and Woodstock just after I left. In contemporary American culture, these two events represented seismic shifts — which others had been absorbing and adjusting to while I was away in Laos and Algeria.

The same senior monk who had orchestrated an attempted sexual encounter with me the year after I graduated from SMC drove me down to Morro Bay (where my parents had bought a small motel while I was away) soon after I arrived back in the States. Why him and why did I attempt to maintain a relationship with him, I'm not clear — except that I know well that many survivors seek to remain in contact with their abusers for myriad reasons; denial and wanting to hold on to the "good" parts of the relationship are two examples. Unfortunately, the abuser often construes continuing engagement as both forgiveness and permission, neither of which the survivor intends.

In Morro Bay, my father was cool to the monk, bordering on rude. I suspect that there was some jealousy involved. He also made clear that I was welcome for a brief visit, but was not moving in — which I had no intention of doing anyway.

It wasn't long before I was camping out with Nick in San Francisco. Having arrived some time before me, he had gotten to know the new San Francisco and was the one who took me to the bar mentioned above. We were initially with friends of friends — then we rented a wonderful older home in South San Francisco — where a childhood friend of Nick's, Sheila, lived with her family two doors down — on Holyoke Street. She was the one who told us about the house being available. Sharon at some point also moved in with us. We three — plus a parrot, a de-skunked skunk, and Sharon's wonderful old soul of a dog, Fritz — made for a very harmonious household — albeit the humans were often stoned.

Jerry from Nice made a brief cameo appearance, and I had my first sexual experience of being a top, with my first male escort, on Holyoke Street — I liked it very much — and also of being a bottom, with a gentle man I had just met, which was OK, but not as enjoyable. There were acquaintances and minor friends who became sexual partners, but I remained hopelessly naïve about actual relationships.

A man whom none of us knew somehow gained entry to the house when Sharon was home alone and attempted to rape her. She was able to fend him off by telling him that if he went through with it, "it will really mess me up." It was deeply painful to learn that she had suffered this insult, and I was not able to protect her.

Holyoke Street was also where I began to understand how alone I was. Not good alone — restorative, meditative, soothing — which I enjoy very much today, but more not-good alone — sad, scared, confused, ashamed. The tumult of my college years and my two years abroad — with their built-in companionship and adventure — were now behind me, and I lacked any sort of clear map for the road ahead — professionally — but also personally, relationally.

After my two years in the developing world, I had to entirely reconsider my perception of the US. At the same time, there was a new gay culture that had exploded during my time away. Did I dare live openly and no longer hide my sexuality?

About this time, Nick's entire family gradually adopted me. I spent many weekends with him at his parents' house in Nevada City. We painted their house, and I was a frequent guest at their table. After Nick's father died, Nick and I spent hours playing Pedro with his mother and her sisters. I was as often the bartender — Manhattans all around — as Nick was. I went with Nick to the hospital, waiting for his mother to be wheeled out after open-heart surgery and, years later, attended her funeral.

We spent time with his two older brothers and their families. We water-skied on Lake Tahoe with one family, and spent evenings at their Reno home with the other. I got to know his four nephews and his niece, Laurie. I'm still in touch today with Laurie and Corey, Nick's oldest nephew, as well as Nick's next-older brother and his wife.

Sheila and her family extended a similar embrace. I always knew that I — and my friends — were welcome in their home. They moved from San Francisco to Rocklin, in the foothills of the Sierra Nevada Mountains, near to where Nick and Sheila had grown up. We enjoyed a great many raucous evenings — and a holiday or two — with them, watching their two daughters grow up over the years. Nick was like a third parent to the girls. We celebrated birthdays and played bocce in the backyard. Sheila and her husband, Mike, are gone now too — but both daughters and I keep in touch.

They all still feel like family to me, even though Nick's been gone more than twenty years. I know I help keep his memory alive for them, and vice versa. I doubt that they fully appreciate the depth and impact on my life of their generous familial embrace.

I attended and/or participated in several friends' weddings. Old friends were moving on with their lives, starting careers and families. It was during this time that word reached me that an SMC classmate had referred to me as a "lost soul," and another as having "gone to pot." I can't honestly say that either characterization was wholly off base. While others moved on with apparent ease, I had a huge, deep fog to fight and figure my way out of. I lived my life in disjointed pieces, compartments; I had no idea how to integrate them into a wholly and healthily functioning being.

A friend from SMC got me a job waiting tables at a steak house in Marin County, and I, in turn, was able to get Sharon and Nick jobs there as well. It was quite a commute from South San Francisco, but served us all well for a time.

I worked in a couple of residential treatment facilities for supposedly emotionally disturbed adolescents who often had been abused in their families and by the juvenile justice system. One, in San Francisco, was populated primarily by African American young people; another, near Sacramento, by White kids. I'm not sure that either population was better served than the other, but the worlds which birthed them could not have been more different. What they did share was their economic class — and their less than nurturant and safe family environments. Few middle- or upper-class kids would have been sent to these institutions; there were private alternatives — with better amenities and staffing — for those who could afford it.

On some levels, I related to all of these young people.

Gay friends teased me that I didn't "trick" (engage in anonymous sex). That wasn't entirely true, but it was true that I strongly preferred sex in connection — I liked to know the other person...at least somewhat. As an Enneagram

4 — hopeless romantic — I was hugely prone to crushes — and years away still from realizing that I was in love with a fanciful notion of love. I liked sex — a lot — but didn't particularly care for it when there was no affection or connection involved — too mechanical, too impersonal, perhaps too reminiscent of my earliest experiences with my father.

Harvey Milk was the proprietor of Castro Camera, one of many openly gay business owners who helped transform the Castro from a sleepy, Italian American, Catholic, working-class neighborhood into the mixed-population "gay mecca" it has since become. Bars and clubs proliferated — Toad Hall was the hippie bar, and my favorite at that time; The Badlands was the leather bar; Twin Peaks and the Elephant Walk were the see-and-be-seen corner bars. The Midnight Sun — owned by a pair of very talented set designers, and where I would later work as a bartender — was a hugely popular spot where men would gather in close quarters in a relatively small space to chat over very loud house music, drink, and cruise one another.

I started a graduate degree in counseling, but decided, about halfway through, that this was too big a leap for me at that time — I wasn't ready — I had too much internal/personal "stuff" to work through. At the top of this list, and vividly illustrating my point — when I was twenty-six, I tried to take my life, and all of the irresolution that lived behind my mask of normalcy broke through to the surface. I was literally unmasked.

I had spent a night in a San Francisco jail, having been arrested at my work after being accused of "contributing to the delinquency of a minor" — I thought I was being helpful. The charges included having sexually abused said minor.

"Eric" (then fifteen) had run away from his home in the Midwest; he called me when he arrived back in San Francisco, saying that he would turn tricks on the street if I did not take him in. I had met him the prior year at a holiday party at his aunt's — a graduate-school classmate — and spent fun, touristy time with him and his family during his visit. We all became fond of one another.

With decidedly mixed feelings, I met him as requested, and we returned to my apartment; I had since moved into my own place. Eric was different from the happy-go-lucky, fun-loving teenager I had met just a few months prior. He was sullen and pale, and extremely angry with his father. I insisted that he call his mother immediately to tell her where he was and that he was OK. I suggested that he invite her to come out to collect him — and offered to mediate a conversation between them if both felt that that would be helpful.

The next day, the father having called the police, Eric was removed from my apartment and taken — furious — to juvenile hall. The day after, the police arrived at my work for me. I was by then tending bar and waiting tables at the Cliff House in San Francisco — where I also met Norma, who became a hugely consequential person in my life.

My boss at the Cliff House very kindly bailed me out the next morning. In the jail, we were six to a cell. The others cheered when my name was called, and I was told, "Bring your blanket." They knew before I did that that meant I was being released; I was the only one. One guy gave me a message for his girlfriend, which I delivered when once again "on the outside." My cellmates had been and would be locked up there for a considerably longer period of time, for different reasons, mostly waiting for court dates. That one night was a revelation and an education in itself.

Gobsmacked, mortified, terrified, bewildered, hurt, and angry at both myself and the situation, I realized too late that I was in way over my head. I found and retained a sympathetic attorney whom I wound up paying in temple rubbings I had brought back from my time in Southeast Asia — as I was a restaurant worker without savings and no other means to pay.

The day of the first scheduled hearing, all charges were dismissed; the father, having decided against pursuing the matter, did not appear. My attorney and I — hugely relieved — sat in the courthouse cafeteria for a while and reflected wistfully on the whole sorry tale — for all concerned. One was, he explained, contrary to popular belief, normally more or less considered guilty, as accused, unless proven otherwise.

Years later, Eric and I briefly crossed paths again, and compared notes on our experiences of that difficult time. He confessed that he had acted as he did to provoke his father. He told me the story of having seduced a man in a hotel lobby between his two California visits; he "got myself fucked." After his second visit to California, he had been sent to a boarding school somewhere in New England to finish high school. I have no idea what has since become of him or his family.

From my perspective, Eric's behaviors and motivations were only part of the story. Albeit caught up in the maelstrom of his family dynamics, at twenty-six, I was the adult, the responsible party. Particularly accustomed to friendships with — and infatuations involving — younger people from my work in various settings, I considered myself responsible for the whole sorry mess, my judgment deeply flawed — in ways that I did not fully grasp at the time.

Years later, when my father was arrested for attempting to molest two neighbor boys, and spent his seventieth birthday in jail, I thought back on this episode — enormously different, but somehow inexplicably the distorted judgment in the earlier one seemed to have been informed by the same root as the later one, a kind of dark inflection and "infection of the psyche" (Jung) of my upbringing.

I identified with Eric and felt drawn to protect him from his angry father. And I felt wholly re-shamed by these accusations and their ramifications. Shaken to my core by the entanglement, I tried to take my life. Medically, the attempt was not particularly damaging, but it left me thoroughly wounded — physically, emotionally, spiritually, and psychologically.

After my attempt, I was required to spend a night or two for observation in a mental health clinic, where it happened that a member of the staff was a former colleague from one of the residential treatment programs I had worked in. He was shocked and saddened to see me there as a patient; I was deeply embarrassed. The attending psychiatrist said that I needed to learn to let go of my "stubborn independence"; little did he know that it was my main mechanism of survival. Another member of the staff told me that I was going to go to hell — which is exactly where I suggested he himself go forthwith.

Nick, great friend that he was, was my rock — compassionate and without judgment — through this period. He and another friend took me for a long drive along the Sonoma Coast, where I remember, through my fog, seeing pelicans swoop in formation above the sea, scolding me with a reminder of life's majesty. I was immeasurably relived to have failed in my attempt, and to still be alive.

After it was all over, I felt in need of a pilgrimage — hoping to find some cleansing, clarity, and direction from what felt like a life shattered anew. I dropped out of my graduate program, sold my car and most of my other belongings, gave up my apartment, and bought a ticket for Ireland.

Before I had fully absorbed my time in Laos and Algeria, I once again departed for foreign lands. Twelve-step program friends would later tell me that I had been "doing geographics" — program talk, I believe, for attempting to escape one's internal reality by constantly changing their external reality — trying to escape oneself. Perhaps they were right — but it's also true that I had moved all my life, loved to travel, and had already begun a pattern of escape from one situation to another when I felt the need; it seemed like quite the natural thing to do.

So I returned to the university of life experience. I had the notion that I would discover my roots, seek communion with my ancestors, heal in solitary wandering. I also left behind any further exploration of the explosion of sexual freedom — and the communities it built — in the San Francisco Bay Area, which had been ushered in by Stonewall.

Amongst what little I carried with me, I packed the *I Ching*, together with three antique Chinese coins in a small

Algerian leather purse, and the *Tao Te Ching*, into which I taped and pasted a variety of photos and drawings of and from favorite people. They were essential and invaluable companions; I still have them both today.

I hitchhiked through much of Ireland, learning only later that I was looking for my ancestors in the wrong places — Cork and points south. Had I known then what I do now, after my in-depth genealogical study, I would have traveled instead north, to County Roscommon, where I could have met the last of my father's direct line, Michael King, who — as I mentioned earlier — was found dead and robbed on a street in Galway, apparently after a night of heavy drinking, much later, in 1988. He was still alive during my visit to Ireland in 1974.

"Loneliness, it eats at you," observed the kind older woman in whose home I had rented a room for the night in Dublin. She had stopped in to offer me some tea and must have read it on my face. Loneliness was then, and had often been, a frequent companion. Her comment reminded me of one made by an SMC faculty confidant to whom I had entrusted my Laos and Algeria journals. When he returned them to me after reading them, his immediate comment was, "Has anyone ever been so alone?"

But onward! I stuck out my thumb on a road heading north out of Dublin, and got a ride with a fascinating pair all the way to Belfast. One was a journalist, the other active with the IRA. I listened from the back seat to their very serious back-and-forth, only able to understand parts of what they were discussing. Once arrived in Belfast — soldiers armed with machine guns on street corners — these guys dropped me at the ferry for Scotland — and told me to keep going, for my own safety, which I did.

From charming, ancient Scotland (my mother's father's family, I learned later, originated from the Isle of Mull), I traveled south through England and crossed the English Channel at Dover, landing at Calais.

Fatefully, one of my first rides in France — which took me both all the way to Paris and deeply into the lives of the car's two occupants — Suzanne and Phillipe, mother and son — grounded my wanderings for a time as I joined their orbit. She was driving; he was in the front passenger's seat; I was in the back. She looked a number of times in the rearview mirror in what I took to be a seductive fashion. His behavior also seemed seductive to me. Was I projecting through my confusedly hypersexual window onto the world? I was rarely certain and had yet to acquire confidence in my judgment in such situations.

Suzanne had just collected Phillipe from a clinic where he had been staying after a bad LSD experience. She and Phillipe's father — a prominent attorney — were divorced. She and Phillipe were in an incestuous relationship.

I wound up staying first with the two of them in her apartment outside of Paris, slightly north of Versailles, during which time I was introduced to Parisian friends, including Nicole, who owned and operated a health-food restaurant in the Montparnasse neighborhood of Paris.

Some of my time in Paris, I stayed as well with friends of Phillipe's who had a magnificent multi-story flat, on the Isle St. Louis, with commanding views of the city from its rooftop

156

terrace. If these folks had offered to adopt me, I might well have accepted.

I remember calling Norma from this apartment. We had been talking about her coming to Paris and our getting married there; she told me in that conversation that this was not going to happen. Instead, she told me, knowing that I preferred men over women, that she had seduced a young man who had no prior sexual experience so that we three might live together as a *ménage à trois* — an arrangement that awaited me upon my return to the States. While I admired her creativity, and had to acknowledge that she was more reality based than I was, I could not see such a thing working for me. So ended my last flirtation with the notion of marriage to a woman. Norma and I would remain in each other's lives — as dear friends — for years to come; I never met her young lover.

Somehow, the Nicole association resulted in Phillipe's and my renting a large seaside house in Saint-Nic, on the Bay of Douarnenez, in Brittany (Bretagne) — well west of Paris — which I remember us accessing through Chartres. It was the spring of 1974.

I had debated staying in Paris on my own and moving on when the time felt right, versus joining Phillipe in the Bretagne adventure. One afternoon, still undecided, I was sitting alone on the banks of the Seine when a large tourist boat appeared under one of the bridges. On the boat's bow was emblazoned its name: BRETAGNE. I saw it as an omen, and I was in.

I spent much of what little money I had at the time buying several doses of LSD from someone Phillipe knew in Paris;

he wrote bad checks for the rent. With Nick and Sharon in California a few years earlier, I had had my first acid experiences, which taught me to respect the drug's potency.

We stayed a month or so in Saint-Nic, Phillipe insisting on a large house because of all the visitors we would have, including a French-actress acquaintance he believed himself to be romantically involved with. We had separate rooms, his downstairs and mine up, with a wonderful large window overlooking the bay. There were also two guest rooms on the second floor.

Our only visitor was Suzanne, who (officially) stayed in one of the guest rooms. The house was old, with a classic huge stone fireplace in the main room downstairs — the source of heat and means of cooking for traditional families in Brittany — and creaky floors. During the nights of Suzanne's stay, I could hear the floorboards creak, and either she went downstairs or he up — I wasn't sure which. After his mother left, Phillipe said quietly, "I still have my problem with my mother."

Before Suzanne's visit, Phillipe and I would walk down to a secluded cove just below where we were staying, and swim and hang out on the beach. We'd also spend quiet, languid hours side by side at a long table in my room upstairs, overlooking the bay, writing. He was writing what he called "Autopsie de Mes 21 Ans" — sadly prophetic, as he suicided in his mother's apartment two years later. And we'd spend some evenings on acid, staring into a large fire we had built in the downstairs fireplace.

On one of our visits to the cove, Phillipe asked me to cure his poor vision. He had obviously developed a nearly delusional ideal of me. During one of our acid evenings, he insisted that I stare at him closely, saying, "You must see" — and, power of suggestion or no, I did see in rapid succession his face in both male and female versions, both beautiful and grotesque, across what seemed like centuries of apparel and expressions — past lives? He thought so.

He was a young guy who imbued the people and world around him with immense powers, perhaps in compensation for his paternal abandonment, helplessness to escape his mother, and, on some level, knowing that he would himself never master the larger world. I came to love him as a little brother and feel protective of him. Ours was an open, affectionate, and intimate relationship, albeit not sexual.

After Suzanne's visit, Phillipe withdrew into a multiday depression. He closed himself in his room; I would rarely see him — though heard his door open and close in the night. During this period, I embraced what I later came to see as the beginnings of my "LSD self-therapy."

One night, on acid, I sat on the ledge of the open upstairs-hallway window — and stared at an eclipse of the moon, during which I felt that I was looking into mysterious celestial realms momentarily revealed by the eclipse — for hours. During another, I sat mesmerized by the magnificent lightning storms that danced and pranced across the entire bay, seemingly just outside my upstairs window. These storms took up the entire field of vision and seemed to go on for hours. I've never seen their equal anyplace else in the world.

Other nights, I built a huge fire downstairs for myself and sat meditatively, all night, watching it burn and change shapes and hues, in which I observed multiple worlds dancing and cavorting before me. Some mornings, after, without having slept, I walked into the nearby village and sat in the small church during the early Mass, in order to stare up at the ceiling's gold stars against a brilliant dark-blue background. A few older women, all dressed in black, and I were the only ones in attendance. One morning, the priest stopped and asked me if I wanted to talk with him about anything, to which I smiled and said simply, "*Non, merci.*"

In retrospect, I can see that LSD was one of many therapies (others include meditation, psychotherapy, and hypnotherapy) that provided me an avenue out of the fog of my early life. It allowed me to see and feel deeply, to find a sacred stillness within myself and in relation to the outer world that had not been spoiled — or even touched — by my parents' darknesses.

It took me a while to recognize that my mother's abandonment was as injurious as my father's more overt abuse. I think now that I had needed to see myself as having had at least one "good" parent who loved and protected me.

On acid, I was somehow able to begin to isolate and contain what had been inserted / imposed from the outside, and to feel, beginning to emerge, a heretofore-unfamiliar sense of wholeness — and possibility. I didn't feel then — and don't now — that I had triumphed over my childhood abuses / demons, but rather that there could be fullness of life despite them — and that they would not destroy me, as they had my siblings.

After Phillipe's and my time in Brittany, I resumed my journey south — to visit friends in Algeria, where I also met up with Nick and his old friend Marti, with whom he was traveling. We enjoyed rich visits with old friends, then hitchhiked east, into Tunisia, where we stayed a few nights in Tangiers before boarding the boat for Rome.

Our last night in Algeria, we slept on a beach not far from the border with Tunisia. We spent the evening with some young Algerians who envied our freedom and ability to travel, as they had neither. I'll never forget them saying to us, as we parted company, "You have to live for us as well." If ever I was aware of my First World privilege, it was in that moment.

We heard the news on that crossing that Nixon had resigned the presidency, so it was August 8, 1974.

We spent a few days in Tunis, then boarded a ferry for Rome, which stopped off in Sicily and ports south. We parted ways in Rome. I had decided that I was ready to return to the States, but, alas, had no money for a return ticket. I traded Marti my camera for the price of my plane ride back.

This time, there was no visit with family and no Greyhound Bus across the country. I did land again on the East Coast and hitchhiked my way across. I slept one night in a field. Some kind persons took me in and fed me for a night. When a pickup truck with others in the back stopped for me when I hit Washington state, and my fellow travelers handed me a joint once I was settled in, I knew that I was home.

It was autumn 1974; I had only been gone a few months, but the journey worked its magic. I had no plan, but was ready to figure out what was next.

Phase 2: Mendocino

Back in San Francisco, I was walking wistfully along with my backpack on, destination unknown, when I saw a silver case on the sidewalk. I picked it up and opened it; it contained some white powder, a syringe, and a bundle of cash. I tossed the powder and syringe, kept the case and the cash, and headed north, by thumb, to the rural and picturesque former lumber town of Mendocino, on the California coast, with which I had long been enchanted — but never visited.

Thus began a rich, memorable, and impactful next phase of my bohemian period.

Early in my time there on the north coast, a beautiful — in body and soul — young man, Michael David — whom I had met in San Francisco and with whom I had spent brief periods of time here and there — came to live with me. I was very much in love with him — but he was absolutely correct that at this moment in time I was not a great prospect for a long-term relationship, as I had no job, no car, and no place of my own. The whole bohemian thing became a fatal obstacle for him in building a future together.

I came back one day to the place we had been sharing (a loft in the garage of some lovely local artists who were kind enough to take us in temporarily) to find a note from him saying that, though he loved me and our time together, it was all too tenuous for him. He had departed; I was heartbroken — but, later, understood.

A couple of friends with benefits from earlier in my life came for brief visits, but my time in Mendocino was otherwise solitary on the romantic front. I had come to welcome, understand, and really enjoy sex just fine, but romance? That still remained a foreign and confounding universe to me.

A friend invited me to cabin-sit for her while away on extended travel. My landlady during those days once commented to me, when she kicked her then boyfriend out, that "we had a flesh-flash and called it love." I knew immediately and exactly what she meant. I easily and frequently mistook infatuation and mutual sexual attraction for love; I had had only scant experience with the real thing in my life. I longed for it — and feared it since I knew it could hurt. It continued to be the case that the greater part of my "issues" was contained within that idealized and seemingly unachievable realm. It took me quite a while to realize that I was deeply reluctant to trust — which, given my multiple experiences of betrayal and abandonment, made perfect sense to me once I "got it."

Later, as I absorbed my professional training and various therapies, including my study of character disorders and psychological diagnoses, I understood myself as longing for relationships that I both feared and could not figure out how to make happen in my life. I then understood how and why different people described me as withdrawn or aloof. Nick once commented to me, with exasperation, "A lot of people want to love you, Neal — if you would only let them." I recognize now traces/hints of a schizoid reality — albeit much less today than in my earlier years.

There were women I met in Mendocino who made clear that they would welcome me as a lover. My experience with Norma, however, convinced me that it was time — beyond time — to admit once and for all that while there were a number of women whom I loved and admired, I would become lovers with none of them. This was an exact re-realization from the first time I had had it in Algeria. The romance front, for me, clearly meant figuring out what it meant to be in an authentically intimate relationship with another man.

"*Il me rapelle d'un grand ami en France*" (he reminds me of a good friend in France), Jacques said to Debbie, his American girlfriend, as they both peered out at me from the open kitchen half door of La Café de la Grange on Mendocino's Main Street, which they owned and managed. I was looking for work. Jacques continued, "*Demande-lui s'il veut faire la vaiselle ce soir, pour commencer*" (ask him if he wants to wash dishes this evening, to begin).

"*Absolument*," I replied, acknowledging that I had understood and was ready to start that evening. I had passed the test — and even spoke French! For the first time since leaving the Cliff House, I had a job.

Jacques was a bit of an outlaw. A mason by trade, he had gone bankrupt in France before he met Debbie there, a fresh, young American tourist. Leaving his three children temporarily behind, he and Debbie landed in Mendocino and opened their café, downstairs from a small inn — which they also managed and where the couple had an apartment. He was not a chef; the menu consisted of the relatively few items he had learned to cook in France — which he cooked very well.

I essentially apprenticed under Jacques — learning how to make his bread, his omelets, his lentil soup, his leg of lamb, etc. Soon, I was opening the café in the mornings, starting the bread dough for that evening, and cooking and serving breakfast. Jacques cooked us all a midday meal, and then it was off to work again, preparing for dinner. It was fun to be back in a restaurant environment...and to be speaking French all together. I had never been in a cooking role in any of my prior restaurant experience, so that part was great fun as well.

That winter, still 1974, Jacques and Debbie returned to France to collect Jacques's children and bring them back to live in the US. In their absence, Monique — a uniquely huge-hearted soul who had lost her parents in the Holocaust and who was herself hidden by a Catholic family in France during the war — and I managed the café. It was a fabulous time. She was older, far more experienced than I, a wonderful cook, and a lot of fun. She lived a few miles outside of town with her writer husband and their two children.

Mendocino at that time was, in part, an artists' colony, and locals lived partly in a bartering economy. At the café, we traded meals for dinner music and cords of firewood. On Christmas, after our few paying guests had finished their dinners, Monique and I kept the café open and invited locals to join us for a holiday feast — our treat. It was a glorious, joyful gathering with wine and music flowing, children cavorting, and a wonderfully festive spirit.

Mendocino also perpetuated in its somewhat off-the-grid way a hippie ethos. We sat around naked together in communal hot tubs, for example. For my twentieth-eighth birthday, I was treated to a many-handed naked massage on the floor of Monique's house. As I recall, my masseurs included Monique, her husband, and at least one of her children, plus Nick and a former student of his, who were visiting at the time. There may have been one or two others. I recall lots of hands.

The cabin was pretty basic. As with many homes there, heat was provided by a wood stove. The local saying was that we heated ourselves twice: once while chopping and gathering the wood, and again when we built a fire from the same wood.

One day, quite suddenly and out of nowhere, as I was out collecting firewood with another local French fellow, Jean-Pierre, and mutual friends in the forest, he literally plopped himself into my life. He came directly out of the forest to me and turned onto his back, his legs in the air, his eyes beseeching. He was an emaciated, young Irish setter, covered with ticks, who had evidently been abandoned — or managed to get lost. My first thought was, *Shit, I have a dog* — something that I had not even considered at that time. But indeed I did, and even though we enjoyed only three years together, there were few dull moments. There could easily be a whole separate volume on our adventures together. As a hint, whenever I picked up my backpack, he leaped into the air and turned circles of joy.

My new companion of course needed a name. While he and I were hanging out in front of the café shortly after he arrived in my life, an endearingly smart-alecky young man who lived just out of town, with his family, strolled past and asked sneeringly, "So what are you going to name him?" The lad's name was Tom, and I had come up with nothing else, so I replied simply, "Tom." The red dog had a name, and the human he was named after beamed from ear to ear.

My time in Mendocino deepened my love of silence — and long, silent walks in nature — into the forest or along the coast. Tom-dog was a frequent companion, running off ahead on his own and then finding me from time to time. Setters are very high energy, so his need to run was a great incentive to get out into those venues. Tom particularly loved running along the headlands, and the memory of him silhouetted against the sunset warms me today. At the cabin, the neighbors' dogs formed a pack; they came to our door every morning for Tom. I let him out — and he'd reappear a couple of hours later, exhausted and happy.

I was lonely and horny much of the time. I tried taking both violin and piano lessons; the metronome drove me nuts, and I concluded that I was tone deaf anyway. Tom hated the violin.

At the café, Tom mostly settled down in the kitchen or in the small yard in back — fortunately, the health inspector never paid a visit during those days. One time, I caught him just as he was about to grab that evening's leg of lamb off the counter. Another, when the landlord none of us liked came by, I had to restrain him as he was barking wildly at the man — who was not amused to see that Tom had joined the café crew.

It was also here that my more-or-less formal meditation practice began — sometimes with others, but mostly solo. I experienced trancelike states and once felt that I was on the verge of levitating — which frightened me away from continuing for a while. And while there were occasionally weed or mushrooms involved, the meditation was mostly unaided.

The embrace of silence and the depth of my meditation practice during my time in Mendocino built naturally upon my times on acid — in silence — with Phillipe on the Atlantic coast of France. Together, they ushered me into a private internal space of safety and sanctuary I could always visit and, when needed, retreat; no one could reach or touch me there. What I later learned was called "mindfulness meditation" became a part of my daily life.

For me, it meant that I could carry my meditation with me and access it at will; there didn't have to be a formal posture or ritual. Little by little, during these years, I found myself building inside myself places of light and calm that helped to push away — or at least balance — the darkness and states of anxiety I had inherited from my early life. This ability to retreat within was different from what I later learned was dissociation — a common survival mechanism for abuse survivors, one in which they essentially leave their body and observe what is happening to them from outside, as a way of not being consumed by the insult of the abuse. I was familiar with that one too; the meditative states, in time, provided a much more welcome escape.

Looking back now, it seems likely that I was unwittingly seeking to emulate my Buddhist monk friends from Laos, who in their playful humility remained my teachers for many years.

My sense of isolation notwithstanding, I felt very much at home in my Mendocino life — and feel a deep nostalgia for it today as I recall it here. Jacques helped me close this chapter with his predictable need to turn angrily on people close to him and push them away. I watched this happen with others and decided that when my turn came, it was time for Tom and me to move on.

Jacques did contribute a few prescient observations, which I have thought about on and off since. One, "*Il n'a pas beaucoup de besoins*" (he — Neal the monk — doesn't have many needs), and another, "*Il est toujours triste, préoccupé*" (he's always sad, preoccupied — a reflection of my never feeling quite whole in my interior life).

I tried leaving Tom-dog with my friend Kati, who waited tables at the café, for a few days while I went south to the Bay Area to look for work and prepare to move. We shut Tom in Kati's cabin and were outside saying our goodbyes, next to the pickup truck I owned jointly with Jean-Pierre, when we heard a loud bang, immediately after which Tom came running from the cabin and wrapped his legs around one of mine, holding tightly. I once again looked into those beseeching eyes. Moments later, contently curled up on the front seat, his head on my lap, Tom had once again won the day — and off we set together.

Post-Mendocino Adventures

Tom-dog and I traveled a lot by road/thumb during our time together — hence my earlier observation at his delight when he would see me pick up my backpack — he knew this meant adventure. He got us lots of rides that I alone would not have scored. One particular memory perhaps captures best the essence of our travel together: We slept one night in a forest; I think in Humboldt County. I awoke from time to time. Sometimes, the red dog was nowhere to be seen; others, he was nestled up snugly against me. Come morning, we both were ready to get back on the road.

Margrethe wanted to see the Grand Canyon. It was her first visit to the USA. So off we all went in Nick's Datsun pickup truck with camper — Margrethe, Nick, Tom-dog, and I. For some reason, Nick and Tom-dog didn't get along. At

169

one overnight camping spot along the Colorado River, Tom-dog found Nick's favorite lilac T-shirt, which he had brought back from Europe, and tore it to shreds — the only time he ever did anything like that.

So Tom-dog and I spent a fair amount of time in the — attached but with no opening to the cab — camper on that trip. When we stopped at the canyon rim, it was approaching sunset, and the magnificence moved us all to spontaneous song. When Nick and I lit up a joint, Margrethe intoned, "Bye-bye." This trip was sometime between Mendocino and what followed.

San Francisco eventually became home again — for a while, Kati and Jean-Pierre from Mendocino and I — with some local friends — tried to start up our own restaurant on Eighteenth Street in the Castro District. We had a great space picked out, but were quickly humbled and rebuffed by the costs of meeting the health department's requirements. We had the talent, but not the resources.

One of the San Francisco participants in our would-be restaurant venture offered to get me a job at the Midnight Sun, a previously mentioned and prominent gay bar on Castro Street. He said it would be "good for me." I wasn't exactly sure what he meant, but was intrigued and needed a job, so applied and was accepted — first as one of the guys who checked IDs, told guys they had to stop whatever sexual activity they were involved in (not allowed — this was a respectable establishment!), and collected dirty glasses and empty beer bottles — and then as a bartender, after having survived my initiation. During the busier hours, the place was packed, body to body — by design.

When I was out on the floor doing what was needed, my hands full of empty glasses and/or bottles, there were often uninvited hands on various places on my body; this is where I perfected "the look."

During this same time, a former DLS student, Tim — a very dear and profoundly good soul — and I ran into each other, started dating, and moved in together — with Tom-dog, of course — first on Twentieth Street, a block up from Dolores Park, and then on Shrader Street in the Haight. Tim was working at a gay bathhouse, the Barracks, south of Market Street, while I continued working at the Midnight Sun. We never ran out of stories to tell away from work.

Tom-dog was used to running free and then finding his way home. One day, at the house on Twentieth Street, there was a knock on the door. I opened it, and there were two police officers with a hugely abashed Tom-dog. He had been down at Dolores Park and gotten busted; he led the officers to the house. We were let off with a warning, but that was the end of Tom-dog's solo trips to the park.

One very busy night at the bar, while I was still on the floor collecting glasses and bottles, a lovely drag queen took pity on me and said, "Open your mouth, honey" — which I did. She deftly popped a hit of acid into my open mouth — and the night became that much more interesting.

New Year's Eve 1975, after I got off work, Tim and I went together to the Barracks, which was quite festive for the occasion. It was like walking into a Fellini film. The punch bowl was a toilet, into which punch flowed from a customized dildo, the liquid shooting up into the air and landing in the bowl — with perfect aim. Most patrons were in their birthday suits for the party; some of the more modest ones wrapped towels around their waists and greeted one another by reaching under the other's towel — rather than shaking hands or a kiss on the cheek. Walking down the hallways, glancing into the private cubicles, one could see almost any imaginable fantasy scenario being played out — slave/master, doctor/patient, etc. Tim and I left, both feeling quite naïve.

At the Midnight Sun in those days, our house music was produced for us and delivered in the flat, square box in which reels of tape were packaged and transported at the time — always with a provocative pornographic photo affixed to the cover for employee enjoyment. The bartenders took delivery and tended the tape player. One shift, I was working with another young bartender who turned the tape box's cover partly in my direction — so we could both see the image attached. "You don't do that, do you?" he asked.

"Not in front of cameras," I replied.

I guess I had a reputation for being on the private/conservative side when it came to sexual expression. And it was — without question — the Wild West of gay sexuality, where literally "anything goes," and the notion of boundaries was quaint at best.

In fairness, the mid-1970s' West was no less wild in the straight community.

So as an environment for a survivor of childhood sexual abuse to get his footing in the world of adult sexuality, it was less than ideal — sex in the community perhaps, more often than not, was casual, anonymous, and with multiple partners. I remained a "tragic romantic" and liked sex with someone with whom I felt at least some connection — and did see sex as a private matter.

Little did either the larger community or I know that these exact predispositions would be influential, if not determinative, when an unexpected killer virus descended upon us just a few years later.

The Patty Hearst trial was going on in San Francisco. It was February of 1976. One day, Tim and I decided to attend.

The sister of a teaching colleague of mine in Algeria (Patricia "Zoya"/"Mizmoon" Soltysik) was a founding member of the Symbionese Liberation Army, or SLA, which kidnapped Hearst and which she later joined. Hearst was kidnapped at age nineteen in the Berkeley neighborhood a block over from where I lived while teaching at DLS. I lived there in 1968–1969; she was kidnapped in 1974.

We were able to get into the courtroom for at least one day of the trial; the senior Hearsts — he was a powerful newspaper publisher — and Patty were in attendance. Outside, there was a good-sized crowd, wanting and waiting to be admitted, we two amongst them. As we waited for the doors to open, I casually scanned the crowd — all ages and genders, mostly White, and one beautiful young man who — we learned — was in town with friends from Dallas.

As my eyes landed on him, I found that his eyes were locked on me. A face-to-face was inevitable; it became another lusty chapter — one, like most, that I did not see coming at all.

Cotati

Gregory's and my meeting in San Francisco blew up Tim's and my tranquil life. There followed, in quick succession, my hitchhiking to Dallas to see Gregory, which cemented the attraction, which led to Gregory withdrawing from his studies at SMU; our taking the VW his parents had bought him back to them in Arkansas, with Margrethe, who was visiting from Denmark, in tow, and dropping her at an airport somewhere.

Gregory and I signed up with an agency to deliver an automobile to the West Coast for the return trip. It turned out to be a big red Cadillac with a white top; we agreed to deliver it somewhere in LA. En route, we drove through native reservations in Arizona. At one point, we gave a ride to some Navajo kids who stuck out their thumbs when they saw the Cadillac approaching. One said, as we climbed the hill to their village, "I'm just going to let this big red car do all the work."

After we let these guys off in their spartan neighborhood, we saw a sign to the Hopi reservation, and turned down the road leading to it, where we met another sign that said something to the effect of "White people stay out — for your failure to obey our laws and your own." That was quite sobering…

Back down on the main road, we continued west as the piebald early evening splendor of the Southwest's open country unfolded in full majesty. We roared through it in awe in our big Cadillac.

That June, we marched together in San Francisco's Gay Pride parade, a first for both of us.

174

Fast-forward: Gregory and I were living in a rented farm-house in Cotati, Sonoma County, together with Sharon and a childhood friend of hers. Tom-dog of course was there as well, as were Willie (an Australian shepherd that followed us home one day and became Gregory's dog) and Fritz (Sharon's dog) — and, somehow, a kitten that tried to nurse from Tom-dog, which he allowed. Occasionally, the dogs would all gang up on the poor kitten and chase her around the house. We'd yell after them, "Don't eat the cat."

We didn't have a car, nor much money. We bicycled or hitchhiked here and there. I cooked at a local eatery in town and, later, waited tables at a Cattlemens steak house in Petaluma, where Sharon also worked as a hostess. I rode my bike out to nearby Sonoma State — where I would eleven years later — unimaginable at the time — join the graduate faculty in counseling — for an evening creative-writing class.

Gregory and I smoked a lot of weed and had plenteous, rambunctious sex wherever and whenever we could. We were together about eighteen months; it was at about the midway point that I realized this was another flesh-flash — more lust than love — and that we would not go the distance. The months thereafter witnessed the gradual disentangling of our lives — but we had quite a lot of fun overall. He was devilishly clever — an actor, singer, and comedian who loved an audience and to entertain, writing original songs and short stories. There were few dull moments.

In November, we rode our bicycles to our assigned polling places and voted in the national election; Jimmy Carter was elected president. Later that month, for Thanksgiving, Roy and Ellen visited, and we had a number of friends over. We constructed a large table out of some sheets of plywood we found and had at least a dozen people for the holiday feast. A joint was passed around between the main course and dessert. Roy pretended he didn't see it; Ellen took a couple of hits.

After dinner, Gregory had the group doing his version of "the antler dance" — people danced around with their hands on either side of their head, pretending they were antlers. He even had Ellen joining in. I had never seen her dance before. She clearly came to love him, and was saddened when we separated. We could not have known that, two years later, she would no longer be with us.

Sharon, Ellen, and I were chatting in the kitchen one morning during that same visit, when Gregory's and my bedroom door opened and out walked Roy, looking very pleased with himself. Behind Roy, I could see Gregory sitting up in bed — looking quite bewildered. It was pretty clear that Roy had just been fondling him in his sleep and that he had startled awake. Between our bedroom and the adjoining one, there was a Jack-and-Jill bathroom through which Roy must have gained entry unobserved.

We three all understood immediately what had just occurred. Roy, walking smugly past, didn't even acknowledge us. Gregory later confirmed that he had been sound asleep when he felt a hand on his genitals — echoes of my childhood. Despite our collective familiarity with Roy's creepy sociopathy, we were all nonetheless shocked at the audacity and sick entitlement of his craven molestation.

Interestingly, looking back, none of us confronted the monster; such was our conditioning at his hands.

History repeating, a neighbor we hadn't met showed up at the door one morning, Tom-dog and Willie (we allowed them to run free) having led him to our home. The gentleman was angry, saying that our dogs had been chasing his sheep, and if he saw them doing so again, he would shoot them. This was our one warning. No more free roaming for those two.

We celebrated Christmas 1976 in the Cotati farmhouse as well; we made ornaments and gifts for one another and enjoyed a sumptuous meal at home. In early January, I turned thirty — which shocked me into realizing that my life had become stagnant…and that I was no longer a kid. Gregory and I had been stoned and carefree during our time together, forming a poor but mostly happy household with Sharon, her friend, and our animals. But turning thirty woke me up and got me focused on doing something with my life. The vagabond/bohemian years had been amazing — great fun and full of adventure, restorative and probably lifesaving — but were not sustainable and did not a full life constitute — at least for me.

It was also at about this time that I heard from Phillipe's mother about his suicide in her flat outside of Paris. This too was very sobering. I was deeply saddened. When Suzanne contacted me in California to let me know, she said that she had forbidden others to speak of her son, but made an exception for me because "Phillipe was happy when he was with you." I suspect that she knew that I knew the reality of their relationship. I was filled with regret that I had not been able to help Phillipe escape — just as I was with Sharon, Ken, and, ultimately, my dear friend and brother from another mother, Nick.

A clear life pattern emerges and repeats: when threatened, finished with a period of time, or not feeling safe, I withdraw into myself and escape — move on to something and somewhere new and different. I see now, in writing these recollections, that I did that in one way or another again and again — a lesson learned while very young.

The abuse survivor often has no physical escape available to her/him, and so escapes internally — dissociates — leaves the body in the moment. My escapes always began with and included withdrawal from what did not feel safe…and physical escape to anther reality whenever possible.

Mardi Gras in New Orleans via Green Tortoise — a private-group bus trip, participants slept on the hollowed-out bus floor, drove through most nights, and stopped off at national parks for meal and bathing breaks — was my solo off-to-think-about-things thirtieth birthday present to myself. The bus was also our home base in New Orleans. It was February 1977 — a year after the Patty Hearst trial. I did face paintings at the festival to make a little pocket change. The group on the bus was a great mix of generations and genders. It was a good trip that provided me with the perspective and clarity I needed.

Springtime brought with it the inevitable dissolution of our little family in Cotati; we scattered in different directions. Sharon and her friend — and Fritz — took an apartment in nearby Sebastopol. Gregory and I returned to San Francisco, where we also separated — I rented an apartment with the red dog on Oak Street, along the panhandle of Golden Gate Park, and Gregory and Willie moved in with friends.

Tom-dog was once again allowed to run free. We took long walks in the park and through the neighborhood, often at night when it was quiet, losing then finding one another. If I didn't see him for too long a time, I'd whistle, and he'd come running — often just to check in — then off he'd go again. When it was time to go home, I put his leash on him, and we headed back to the apartment…without complaint.

Nick moved in — not planned. He had returned to teaching at DLS, and somehow it did not go well…and he was dismissed. This was one of several times over the years in which one of us bailed out the other. He had stuff — furniture, etc., of which I had little — so Tom-dog and I shared a mattress on the floor on the back porch, where Tom-dog always insisted on his own pillow and laid his head next to mine; Nick had the bedroom. Nick and Tom-dog got along fine during this period.

I didn't have a plan for what came next. Into that void — in the guise of a newspaper ad for a school-counselor position at the American School in London (ASL) — my next chapter presented itself. I answered the ad and was invited to an interview with the headmaster at a bar at the SF airport. I borrowed Norma's car and drove over, telling her I imagined the whole process taking not more than a couple of hours. About four hours later, I returned her car to her — with my apologies — but also with a job offer, made on the spot, after a few drinks and at least a couple of hours of conversation. And, just like that, my vagabond years came to an end.

My starting salary for the 1977–1978 school year was $14,400, plus full benefits — which included one round-trip economy ticket home every other year.

The school was actually three schools — lower, middle, and upper — under one roof. In the upper school, the headmaster said there was a substantial group of students (stoners, artists, outliers) who extant staff was failing to reach and relate to. He felt that I would be able to fill that gap.

I was mostly ecstatic — back to a school environment and a new adventure living in London. However, it meant leaving Tom-dog behind — which brings tears to my eyes even today as I write this. I left him with Sharon and her soon-to-be-husband — who married during the time I was living in London — telling myself he'd be there when I got back, and we could carry on as before. Even I knew that that was a long shot.

My last glimpse of Tom-dog was his head shooting up and looking over to where I stood as Sharon pulled away from the Oak Street apartment — and he realized that I was not coming with them. Tom-dog was a handful — one of many ways in which he and I were well matched; his energy and spirit were too much to ask most others to embrace. His was simply one of the most magnificent spirits I have ever encountered.

Before long, Sharon found a family — near to them in San Luis Obispo County — who took Tom-dog on the condition that I never be told where he was. I understood, but my heart was heavy.

I wound up spending the next three life-altering years in London. Home on a visit, riding in the back of someone's pickup, pulling onto a freeway on-ramp in San Luis Obispo, in a yard, I saw a red dog playing with some children. He was wearing a green collar like the one Tom-dog was wearing when we parted. I yelled, "TOM!" as loud as I could as the truck moved forward. The dog turned in my direction and froze, as if he were listening to the wind. I'd like to think it was indeed Tom-dog — and that he knew then that I had not forgotten him.

Nick kept the apartment. I had no car to sell and few belongings, so packing for London was pretty simple, compared to other departures for foreign lands. My most valuable possessions this time around were the ones that only I knew and understood, the ones that represented enormous work on my part — spirit, will, stubborn iconoclastic independence, curiosity, heart, and determination to live life to its fullest.

Section Two

Reentry and Transformation

We've spent my vagabond years and early adulthood swimming in the muck and overall confusion from my childhood. Throughout, something inside was driving me toward integration and healing, insistent that I seek to reclaim what had been stolen and to fix what had been broken.

At the same time, I'm a socially awkward soul — not sure where or how I fit in, or even how exactly I'm supposed to figure that out.

We'll visit the various sorts of healing remedies that I explored. You'll learn with me that it's at best an imperfect enterprise with a great deal of trial and error, hit and miss.

Part III

Back to School

Chapter Ten
London

Orange — bright orange — was the color of the headmaster's BMW sedan — which he had loaned me to carry my meager brought-with-me-from-the-States belongings from my hotel to the "garden flat" the school had recommended I rent on Abercorn Place, St John's Wood, London NW8.

Little did I know that that seemingly simple gesture would place me, in the eyes of the school community at large, within the extant social dynamic — a single young man from San Francisco, hired and brought to London by the married-with-children, but known-to-be-bisexual head-master, whose car he is now borrowing.

Vera Valentine was my landlady on Abercorn Place, occupying the handsome home above my flat. She created and maintained a prize-winning rose garden — which I appreciated daily outside the French doors leading from my bedroom thereto, and which had been recognized by a visit from the Queen Mother Elizabeth I herself — which visit Ms. Valentine confessed to me rendered her a "nervous wreck." It was fall 1977.

My commute to campus was a five- to ten-minute walk: left on Abercorn Place, then another left across Abbey Road (of Beatles fame — Abbey Road Studios were two blocks away; Paul McCartney lived nearby), then right on Langford Place to Loudoun Road…and voila! As forecast, we were three schools under one roof — lower (K–6), middle (7–9), and upper (10–12).

Assigned to the upper school, I joined a counseling department of three other full-time counselors: one assigned primarily to the lower school, one to the middle school, and the third, like me, to the upper school. We all covered as needed for one another.

In the upper school, we officially focused on academic and college counseling, though invariably personal and family counseling became a focus of our work as well. We were assisted by two part-time learning specialists. I'd estimate that the total enrollment at the time, all grades, was plus or minus 1,000 students. Our students were overwhelming Americans from corporate and diplomatic families, most of whom moved from assignment to assignment around the world.

The lifestyle, which could seem glamorous, was hardest on the moms. The dads had their work, and the kids had school; the moms had to figure it out, and were often lonely.

Cases of sodas were stacked in my office, just behind the door, when I arrived. The husband of one of the other counselors popped in from time to time — whether I was alone or with a student or parents, it didn't matter — to retrieve some of the sodas. I thought the arrangement curious until I realized that he/they felt that I needed monitoring.

I understood even better when I had to chase the same gentleman out of confidential student files — always of comely male students. He taught in the middle school and had no business in those files. I later learned that he had quite the reputation amongst his peers. Thanks to him, I got a massive lesson in projection.

The beneath-and-outside-the-handsome-brochure dynamics of the school gradually continued to reveal themselves. I landed socially in a lovely group of teachers, all American, all 10-plus years my senior, and all close with the headmaster — which included Suzanne, a former nun and talented calligrapher who, despite my having come out to her when we first met, told her students — and some of our mutual friends — that we were lovers. We did become great friends notwithstanding.

There was the gracious and generous life-of-the-party, not-completely-out gay couple — Ray, who taught in the middle school, and Jerry, who taught in the lower school — who drove in their yellow VW Beetle, Vera Charles, from their elegant flat on Hamilton Terrace to the school each morning, Jerry depositing Ray a couple of blocks away so colleagues would not discern that they were a couple. Of course, everyone knew.

Jerry always called me the ingenue of the group. We enjoyed many fun times together in different combinations — dinner parties at one another's flats, concerts, operas, ballets, restaurants, travel. They all were there before and after my three years amidst them, so I must have been something of a friendly visitor, passing through. Ray and Jerry's flat was party central — Jerry in the kitchen and Ray as maître d' — endearingly serving copious drinks and hors d'oeuvres.

Suzanne once observed that I tended to wear loose-fitting clothes and encouraged me to consider more form-fitting attire, saying that I had a "nice figure." I hadn't thought about it then, but understand now that, like many survivors of childhood sexual abuse, I instinctively sought to not attract attention to my body. It was simply safer that way.

I was assigned the tenth grade my first year and dutifully set about contacting each member of that class to acquaint myself and review their class schedules. We all would graduate together three years later. It wasn't hard to identify the students the headmaster had talked with me about during my interview. They were the outliers — some highly creative, some merely high; I loved them.

An odd feature of the school layout had the teachers' lounge and the students' smoking area sharing a glass wall, with a rarely used glass door between them. The effect was that — from either and both sides — one group could look in on the other as if they were in a fishbowl. It was quite amusing. "My kids" (in reality I worked across groups with all students — it was just that these kids were no longer without an adult advocate and friend) were often to be found in the smoking area; I was the only one, that I can recall, actually using the glass door to go from one population to the other — which was initially shocking to my colleagues, while novel but more or less welcome and entertaining to the students.

Daily, lovely campy, middle-aged Andrew served us all afternoon tea — with milk was the default, which took a bit of getting used to. The sound of him rolling his tea trolley your way signaled without fail that midafternoon had arrived. He was always upbeat, full of "hello, loves" and "there you are, dears," often with a flirty twinkle in his eye — everyone loved him.

Amongst the faculty, I was seen as left of center, a California leftie — our more-to-the-right colleagues and

I respectfully in open disagreement on several issues — much to the delight of the students.

The students had decided that I was bisexual — and that that was "cool." Though out to my peers, I had not discussed my sexuality with the students. I kept a book on LGBTQ youth on the bookshelf in my office; those who needed to see it saw it without fail — most were oblivious to its presence.

I was rumored to have been sexually involved with various persons at the school. One young teacher in the lower school concocted a bizarre attempt to lure me. I don't think today that all this was about my inherent animal magnetism, rather to my being a fresh, young presence in an unmoored expatriate community afloat in adolescent hormones...and imagination.

"Baseball coach" was one title I never imagined in my life being attached to me...but...there was a team whose members all wanted to play, but no coach. The students asked if I would become their coach. I advised them that I knew virtually nothing about baseball and almost as little about coaching, but said I'd do it if they were really that desperate — which, evidently, they were. I don't recall it being a particularly memorable season for any of us, but at least they got to play.

On one of my summer visits home to California, I found that Sharon and Eugene had gotten themselves married somewhat spontaneously — and saw, for the first time, the small motel that my parents had purchased and managed on the central coast in Morro Bay. Both were seismic events in the you-can't-go-home-again sense.

It was here that Roy returned from one of his driving trips back to Iowa with a young boy in tow — perhaps a hitch-hiker? I'm not sure. Roy reportedly, on bended knee even, beseeched the boy to remain there with him. Ellen moved out for a short while in disgust and desperation (she had adopted the as-long-as-I-don't-have-to-see-it frame of mind by this point), but returned shortly thereafter, seeing no other viable path for herself alone. The boy evidently did not accept Roy's invitation.

It was also here that Roy's second Fred entered the picture — as the twelve-year-old son of a disabled neighbor in Morro Bay. Roy befriended the boy and entered shamelessly into a sexual relationship with him, which further demolished Ellen.

Ski trips to the Alps were a part of the culture of the London school's winter break. Most were organized and chaper-oned by faculty, a week or two in duration, all expenses paid for the chaperone — in return for taking responsibility for the students on the trip. Early in my first year at the school, I was approached by a senior girl who said that a group wanted to ski Tignes — in the French Alps — that winter, but needed a faculty chaperone — was I available? I happened to be free, so agreed. We'd fly as a group to Geneva, then bus to the resort.

I didn't really know how to ski at that point, so spent my first couple of days in private lessons, determined to par-ticipate in a student's sweet-sixteen party later in the week — which involved skiing to a nearby village for a group lunch. My instructor, very cleverly, when she felt that I could fly solo, bid me adieu at the top of one of the lifts and wished me a good stay as she skied away. I did participate in the birthday celebration.

Val-d'Isère was the location of my last ASL ski trip, where we occupied almost all of a small hotel in the village. On this trip, a different senior girl dared me to hang glide off the side of the mountain — with a pilot, on skis. I said I would if she would. Riding up in a chairlift, I saw her taking off in the hang glider and thought, *Damn, now I have to do it too.* It was amazing.

Two boys who had confided in me that they were a couple asked if it was OK for them to put their mattresses together on the floor of their shared hotel room during the trip. I told them that I considered this a private matter between the two of them.

One evening, the whole group disappeared — nowhere to be found — after some had failed to show for dinner. My fellow chaperones and I went door-to-door in the hotel until we found those who had not appeared for dinner — and all the others — gathered in one of the rooms. It was clearly a party; my observation was that some were stoned, some had been drinking, and a couple were on acid — the ones who had not shown at dinner. We adults regrouped in the hall to confer, then reentered the room — reminding the group of the terms they had agreed to and the legal strictures they were violating. Again, a stern warning — and no similar incidents for the duration.

On another ski trip, a student came by my room one night and started to climb into my bed; I gently told him he needed to return to his own. Despite my experience in Algeria, it still surprised me when students, even some of the younger ones, made the occasional sexual overture — not a frequent occurrence, but more than once.

I did — not unlike in Algeria — allow a couple of recent graduates to share my bed. After one of these trysts, there was mutual regret…and remorse. It should not have happened; I should not have allowed it to happen. Even though consensual and legal, today I would make a different decision, given my since-gained understanding of the power dynamic in the student-teacher relationship.

Sharing a particularly long ski lift one magnificent afternoon in the French Alps, a student honored me with a troubling confidence. Sixteen or seventeen at the time, she was involved in an affair, which had been ongoing for some time, with a married faculty member. She swore me to secrecy — and clearly needed the catharsis. It was of course awkward to engage afterwards with this colleague as if I did not know about the relationship — and to see other students openly captivated by him. He did possess a certain charisma.

She and I met again over thirty years later — she then was married, without children — and took a long walk together. She had told no one all these years about this relationship, but realized as an adult that she had been groomed by this man for a number of years (she was one of several who had been in the middle school before moving to the upper) and remained rightly enraged that he had "stolen my innocence." I was deeply saddened at her enduring scars.

By today's standards, and with my training and ethical responsibilities as a psychologist, I would of course have been required to report this relationship to the appropriate authorities — and would have done so without hesitation.

Years later and after the fact, another student mentioned that a different teacher had hit on him during his ASL years, dismissing it as "no big deal."

At ASL, as at every school I served in, the vast majority of faculty and staff were fine and talented professionals dedicated to their students' well-being in every way. There were always bad apples who seemed to receive a disproportionate share of attention.

My mother, Ellen Ann, was the first of our nuclear family to pass away. I received a call at my flat in London from Roy, my father, saying that if I wanted to see her before she died, I should return to the States right away. He cautioned that she was slipping away and might not recognize me. I was pretty sure she would recognize me — and was just electing not to recognize him. Sharon, who was visiting her regularly, agreed.

This being an unexpected and unbudgeted trip — it was late fall 1978; I had been home to California the prior summer and was living on a school counselor's salary — I took a loan from my local bank and bought my round-trip ticket. I went pretty much directly to see her in her windowless hospital room at Vandenberg Air Force Base, near Lompoc, California.

She was delighted to see me, though clearly only partly "there." Hooked up to various tubes and wires, machines beeping, she was disoriented and a bit delirious. At one point, she indicated a second bed in the room and said that "you and Gregory" can sleep there — Gregory being my former boyfriend of whom she was quite fond. At another point, she offered me one of her wires or tubes; I declined, but thanked her.

I sat for a bit with her attending physician in his office on the floor below her room. He indicated that they were struggling to stabilize her from her various medical conditions (diabetes, cirrhosis, hepatitis — she was quite jaundiced — and perhaps a recurrence of the breast and lymph cancer for which she had received a simple mastectomy a year or so earlier) in order to determine what treatment was possible. I reminded him that she had directed that she not be kept alive on machines, if it came to that, and that the family supported her wishes.

As I was leaving her room for the last time before returning to London, I turned at the door and looked back at her. She was smiling brightly at the attendant standing by the side of her bed. She always seemed to like hospitals (I am the exact opposite), I suspect because of the attention and care she received there.

Ten or so days after returning to London, I received another call from my father, one evening, to tell me that my mother had died. Her request of no life-prolonging interventions had been honored; she wished to be cremated. I asked my father to keep her ashes so that I might spread them when I was home again the next summer. He refused, saying that he'd already made arrangements with the crematorium.

I always understood that cruel gesture as his final dig at her — and me, as her favorite. And yet, for reasons I'll discuss later, I never did fully banish him from my life.

I wept alone in my flat that evening for the small-town New England factory-foreman's daughter who unwittingly married a monster — who was actually smitten with her brother — at eighteen, still a child herself, then became the constantly-in-motion navy wife who had three kids, each born in a different state — by the age of twenty-five — and got swallowed up by the big, cruel, indifferent world, with no safe harbor of her own.

I wept for how sad her life had been, for knowing that I'd miss her, her clear unhappiness notwithstanding, and for all the living she had never gotten to enjoy. I had had visions of her coming to visit in London and taking her to a performance at Covent Garden, just to see the look on her face (I don't believe that she ever owned a passport). I had long before forgiven her for being the decidedly less-than-perfect mother that she was.

In my father's papers was a letter from the hospital where my mother died, dated four days after her passing, showing 243 days of hospitalization there from April 1971 until her death seven and a half years later. She had been in compromised health for some time — much more than I realized.

I'm grateful as I write today that my father called and alerted me to my mother's imminent demise, something I recognize he did not have to do. My mother died, so far as I know, alone in that same hospital room on November 12, 1978, just before 7:00 p.m. She was fifty-three years old.

Recently, I found a poignant letter from Florence, Ellen's mother, written to me on 4 December 1979 — just over a year after her daughter died — and five and a half years after her beloved Wilmot had died. She says of my mother, "She was a good girl, and I loved her deeply, and don't think she was happy for a long time. Maybe she had some of this sickness for a long time..." Before closing, she notes, "Jean and Gordon are very good to me..." and "is so lonesome when you live alone."

By the time my mother died, I had moved from St John's Wood to a wonderful flat in Hampstead — the old servants' quarters above a huge brick mansion on the corner of Frognal and Church Row, London NW3. The house was owned by a Dutch family whose three young sons were students at ASL's lower school. The wife/mother, Tanya, was a decorator, so the flat was beautifully appointed. It had a large outside terrace facing over Frognal, which my landlords allowed me to have fitted with a deck for sitting and sunbathing.

So Hampstead was home for years two and three. I could walk to the village shops, the Hampstead tube station, Hampstead Heath, and my new "local" pub. My commute did become more complicated, requiring a bus down and up Finchley Road, a walk down and up Frognal Lane to Frognal, then left to my corner. A right would have taken me to University College School, also on Frognal. Life became a lot easier when I purchased a used bright-orange VW Beetle; I also became the household chauffeur for all of us headed to ASL each day.

Alternatives was an all-upper-school program, each spring, in which faculty proposed and organized an activity, and students signed up according to their interest. Some stayed in London and visited museums, or went to and studied Shakespeare plays; others explored different parts of England; some went to countries on the Continent.

The two I remember organizing were a rock-climbing expedition in Wales — where I unintentionally demonstrated for the group how one falls from the side of the cliff, is caught by the ropes to which one is attached, and bounces right back to where one started — and after a particularly brutal winter in London, a camping trip to the South of France, near Saint-Tropez.

Both were successful trips. On the latter, my co-organizer, Kay — an Australian colleague and friend who tutored at the school — and I shared a tent platonically — but of course the kids saw what they wanted to see.

The campsite was walking distance to the beach; staff prepared and served all of our meals. We arrived, in early afternoon on a glorious spring day, and told the kids that after they set up their tents, they could walk down to the beach for a few hours' release from the long bus ride from London and to enjoy the spectacular Mediterranean until dinnertime. Kay and I stayed behind to tend to all the administrative details, then walked down ourselves to join the students.

The path to the beach wound through fields of what I recall as being bamboo, quite tall. Kay and I noticed, as we walked along, men amongst the stalks on either side and occasionally crossing the path in front of us. Some of them appeared to be naked. When we reached the beach, lo and behold, there were quite a number of naked men — including, as we strolled up the shoreline, a small group of our male students who, upon seeing the two of us approach, yelled out to me to retrieve and toss them their bathing suits, which were languishing ignored on their towels. I of course complied, and we all had a good chuckle.

As it set in that we'd landed upon a gay nude beach, Kay and I wondered together about how quickly the school would fire us, and the girls on the trip complained that all the men were looking at each other — not fair!

One of the junior boys on the trip was, pretty obviously to Kay and me, openly flirtatious with a male member of the campground staff. We saw no indication that anything came of it during the trip. He was a new student to the school that year, and most did not know him well; he transferred out the next year, moving with his family to where his father's oil-company job took them next, where he completed his senior year.

After his graduation, I received a letter from him (way pre-Internet) saying he was planning to come to London for a visit to see friends and asking if he could stay at my flat during that time. He did…and during his stay commenced what would become a decade-long, on-and-off sexual friendship. He visited me several times during my graduate studies at Berkeley; we enjoyed a delightful, long ski weekend in the Lake Tahoe area, and he attended my fortieth birthday party with his then girlfriend, whom he later married. We're still in touch today, and while not close, we both appreciate our shared history…and shared slightly warped senses of humor.

Looking back, I'd say ours is a relationship made possible and allowed by that particular circumstance and moment in time — and otherwise would likely not have existed. Older, wiser me, even a few years later, would have welcomed the friendship, but without the sex part. Interestingly, at the same time, it endured and acquired a depth and substance over time that my flesh-flash relationships did not.

We had the bus and driver at our disposal for the duration of our trip, so we organized a side trip — along the Mediterranean to Monaco and back, stopping here and there for photos, snacks, and a dip in the sea. We had a system for making sure we were all on board before the bus set off from each stop: each person was responsible to vouch for the person after them on the alphabetical list of those on the trip. This worked well — except when it didn't.

We took off minus one student from one of our stops on the Monaco loop; evidently, the boy ahead of him on the trip had smoked a joint laced with heroin before we set out — and became oblivious to everything external, including the list. Luckily, the missing lad's seatmate proclaimed his absence, and we turned the bus around, finding him standing — decidedly unamused — in the spot where the bus had been parked. Kay and I reinforced the role and importance of the list and, had there been a practical way to do so, would have sent heroin-boy home on the spot. Instead, he was treated to an unwelcome closeness of supervision the rest of the trip, admonished on the dangers of his activity, and advised that there would be further action taken once we were all back in London.

As our trip concluded, we gave the students a choice: one more day on the beach and then drive straight back to London overnight...or...leave the beach the last morning and stop off in Paris, where all could have an afternoon to wander while Kay and I found a restaurant for all to enjoy a final meal together before heading back toward the English Channel.

Paris was the overwhelming choice. We had the bus driver do a quick tour of the inner city to point out landmarks to orient the students; bought several maps of the city, which they took as they prepared to set off in groups; and parked the bus behind Notre-Dame cathedral, which was to be our before-dinner rendezvous. Every student reported back at the appointed time; dinner was delicious and delightful, the perfect finale to a memorable excursion.

Anna Freud, then in her early eighties and nearing the end of her life, presided at the Hampstead Clinic founded by her famous father. I had to sit for a couple of interviews — during which I was told with surprising candor that they all were waiting for Anna's death so they could implement changes from what her father had left behind — before being accepted as an attendee at one of the clinic's lecture series. My work as a counselor working with young people was the ticket to admission. I don't recall the content of the lectures, but will never forget the small circle of white-haired heads bobbing in unison, facing the lectern as Ms. Freud spoke. This was an image that was very present a few years later when I was a doctoral student reading the Freuds.

Ken and my father both visited — separately — in the year after my mother's death; Sharon did not visit me in London, the notion strongly discouraged by her very controlling husband. Ken was generously received by my friends and enjoyed playing tourist. My father and I made a trip over to Paris, during which we visited Phillipe's mother, Suzanne — a bizarre intersection of worlds wherein I was left attempting to translate. Ever brazen, my father commented on the boys he found attractive when we visited the school — he had long since ceased pretending. Margrethe also visited briefly during this time and remembers seeing my father there.

Hans, yet another flesh-flash, also came over for a lengthy visit the fall after my mother died. I had met him the prior summer at Nick's, and we fell immediately in lust. Suzanne, with high drama, bemoaned having been cast aside for my "imported lover," but wound up with egg on her face when our circle of friends learned that her and my love affair had never progressed beyond her imagination. Ray and Jerry were enamored of Hans and very generous. One of their friends was absolutely smitten and invited Hans over to do "odd jobs," so he could ogle him and feed him fresh-baked cookies — and who knows what else — fidelity not being one of Hans's strong suits, just as integrity was not for the other guy.

Hans and I spent Christmas in Paris — with a favorite student and his father — including Christmas Eve Mass at Notre-Dame and an elegant dinner at a very fine restaurant chosen by the father, where we were all his guests.

Hans's visa in my London life expired shortly after that trip — our last hurrah — and he returned to California. My lust-love discernment had obviously not improved; it would have been better to leave our entanglement as a simple summer fling.

Russia in winter — echoes of *Dr. Zhivago* — with Ray and Jerry, two friends of theirs from California, and Suzanne — took the place of what might otherwise have been a final ski trip with students. We rented heavy fur coats. My copy of *The Russians* by Hedrick Smith was confiscated by customs agents upon arrival in Leningrad — which Ray provocatively called Stalingrad for our guides' non-bemusement. Guides asked if they could borrow my copy of *Newsweek*, which had not been confiscated. By the time it was returned to me, it was well worn — my guess is that it had been passed from hand to hand and that many eyes had perused this forbidden periodical.

People on the streets and working at museums asked for chewing gum and blue jeans. The shelves were nearly bare in the grocery stores. Elderly women swept the streets in their babushkas. We took the train to Moscow, through snow-clad villages where folks moved from place to place by snowshoe and cross-country ski.

In Moscow, we enjoyed a performance of the Bolshoi Ballet and spent an evening at a restaurant/dance club where the clientele was comprised of Westerners and upper-crust Russians. There were military officers dancing with abandon in their dress uniforms. We drank delicious Russian vodka as if it were wine.

When the bill came, Suzanne — more than a little tipsy — was outraged at the total and marched into the manager's office, the rest of us discouraging this behavior to no avail. I recall standing behind her in that office as she berated the man in charge, trying to extract her before we all got arrested. One could see Red Square out the office window. Eventually, we got Suzanne to back off, paid the bill, and escaped into the frigid night.

There was abundant other travel. On free weekends, I ventured away from London into the countryside. Venues included the Cotswolds; Kent, where I visited Thavisak, a former student from Laos — who was a great friend of Soupho's — and his family, who had managed to escape the Pathet Lao and were settled in as refugees there; and any coastal area I could reach — often on my own — just to explore and get to know the country better.

It was during one of my final trips to Brittany on the Continent, with Kay and other colleagues, that I ultimately made the decision to leave ASL, after my third year there, and return to graduate school. I had been deliberating for some time, going back and forth.

While I loved ASL, the students, and my life in London, I realized several things: the students were staying the same age, and I was not; some of the "lifers" at the school occasionally seemed as if they felt trapped; I had good instincts working with students and their families, but lacked formal training; I had never to that point seriously challenged myself intellectually/academically. So it was time. I could easily have stayed on and one day retired from ASL, but it simply was time.

There were several farewell gatherings with colleagues and students. I left feeling appreciated and fondly sent off. Suzanne was an exception, warning me that she had had a friend who earned a doctorate and became a psychologist and had been very unhappy since, implying that I would be better off staying where I was.

At the same time, in my personal/private/internal life, I knew that I remained unresolved in fundamental ways — especially in the key areas of intimacy and discernment — that were obstructing my living as a fully functioning and integrated human being. I didn't see remaining in London as likely to change that.

Those I had known as students during my years in London are now in their sixties — most with families of their own, some with young grandchildren. I stay in touch with several on social media, and we enjoy the enduring connection; several have stopped by for a visit when their travels bring them nearby.

My closest ASL colleagues are almost all gone now: Ray and Jerry from COVID; Suzanne from a fall at her home; Jack, the headmaster, from old age. Left is lovely Helen — we are each other's sole remaining witness to these remarkable times. I've lost touch with Kay, who returned to her native Australia.

Chapter Eleven
Berkeley

I had my sights set on UC Berkeley and a doctorate with which I could concentrate on working with adolescents through the arts. In order to apply as a state resident — and see if my then thirty-three-year-old mind could reengage academically — I first spent a year in Sacramento — taking art-therapy and abnormal-psychology classes at Sacramento State while figuring out how best to navigate the admissions process at the university…and waiting tables to pay the bills.

I stayed with Nick, at his place in Auburn, while getting myself situated in Sacramento. Hans too was nearby; I saw him occasionally, and we wound up working together at a restaurant in Sacramento, so I somewhat had the sense of coming home.

Once I was accepted at Berkeley, Hans — ever the charmer — became disdainful — echoes of Suzanne in London — accusing me of "leaving all your friends behind to go become a doctor."

My BA is in English; I had no academic foundation in psychology. I learned that acceptance into a doctoral program pretty much required first establishing a relationship with a faculty member who would sponsor your research. I didn't even attempt the clinical-psychology program, in which the students were the best of the best, straight out of psychology undergrad, destined for careers as psychological researchers at the best universities. I thought that the counseling-psychology program in the School of Education was likely the best fit for my background and interests. Its degree met California's requirement as academic credentials for licensure as a psychologist.

It took a few twists and turns, but that's where I wound up. To gain admission, I was initially sponsored by a professor in the anthropology-of-education specialization — whose work I genuinely found fascinating — but which could not get me where I needed to go. The former dean of the School of Education was a philosopher named Jim Jarrett, who — though not himself a psychologist — was a scholar of Carl Jung, to whose work I was very attracted. I signed up for Jarrett's Jung course, and determined to write a paper that would get his attention, with a view of then asking that he sponsor my transfer into my target program.

My plan worked. One of the lovely things about the since-defunct counseling-psych program is that we students — who were mostly older — with some years out in the world behind us were free to essentially sculpt a program — with advisor consent — from different academic departments that facilitated one's research. I was able to blend and integrate work in clinical psychology, sociology, social work, and education — which was an ideal mix for me.

Individuation is a Jungian term I have come to love; it's essentially the lifelong process of becoming one's true and unique self. It's each of our true vocation — the most fundamental dictate of our being — we are called to it. In Jung's thinking, this is a never-ending process in which no one actually reaches any kind of destination. It includes working to bring the unconscious into consciousness, exposing/revealing and then integrating the "shadow" — thereby diminishing its power — and daring to follow unfaltering allegiance to authenticity — no matter how far out of the bounds of convention your journey might take you. From a bell-curve perspective, individuation is a process that by definition results in an outlier existence far from the bulging center of the curve. Jung believed that most of us get stuck in the gravitational pull of normalcy — and don't get very far in our process of individuation.

Another gift from Jung — enormously liberating for me — was his observation that the human psyche is both contradictory and paradoxical. Thanks to Jung, I felt a little less crazy — things didn't always have to make sense — and I became more and more comfortable holding opposing points of view at the same time.

I had no idea at the time how utterly transformative and determinative my time at Berkeley would be on so many levels; what I learned both academically and about myself reset my entire life.

My eventual dissertation wound up having nothing to do with working with adolescents through the arts. Instead, it was a qualitative treatise — unusual for a research university like Berkeley. Using case-study methodology, I critiqued traditional theory in psychology as narcissistically rooted in the life experience of heterosexual European men — and then generalized it as the norm for psychological health to all populations — and therefore inherently biased against those whose realities did not comport: women, non-Europeans, what we now call LGBTQ folk, etc. — pathologizing these populations, in the process, for deviating from the theorists' subjective norm.

I proposed instead a theoretical Jungian developmental model that was idiosyncratic — rooted in the client's particular life experience — that did not make assumptions based on gender, culture of origin, sexuality, etc.

Jim Jarrett chaired my dissertation committee. Phil Cowan — a Piaget scholar who was on the clinical-psychology faculty — and Paul Heist — a very creative psychometrician who I believe worked in both the clinical and counseling programs — also honored me with their membership on the committee.

Heist introduced me to the concept of "tolerance for ambiguity" as a key indicator of psychological health — one of the scales of his Omnibus Personality Inventory.

There was at that time — 1981–1985 — a relative dearth of diversity amongst the faculty, as is reflected in my homogenous, albeit enormously brilliant and talented, dissertation committee — all straight, White males. I was fortunate, notwithstanding, given my freedom to draw broadly across disciplines in my academic program, to be able to work with a richly diverse group of professors during my research.

My initial sponsor in the anthropology-of-education program was an African American woman. I sought out and worked closely with a brilliant Asian American woman in the social-work department who helped me develop an understanding of the developmental ingredients of character disorders — which were believed by many at the time to be immutable — as well as the impact and consequences of trauma at different developmental stages...and the relationship between the two.

As part of his graduate seminar in Third World psychology, Phil Cowan required participants to also serve as teaching assistants for undergraduates undertaking the same exploration. Meanwhile, the focus of our seminar was an attempt as a group to conceptualize a single psychological paradigm that encompassed our diverse realities: men and women; Jew, Gentile, and other; gay and straight; African American, Asian, and Hispanic. We were a small group and worked diligently toward our goal, but ultimately did not succeed.

Our efforts were written up jointly as a chapter in the 1988 American Psychological Association publication *Teaching a Psychology of People: Resources for Gender and Sociocultural Awareness* — which also includes, as a different chapter, my first solo professional publication, "Teaching about Lesbians and Gays in the Psychology Curriculum."

The university's Counseling Center had a program specifically for LGBTQ students, under the leadership of Bill Merriweather, an out gay psychologist who also served as a member of my orals committee. I worked in this program — with individuals, couples, and groups — as both a pre- and postdoctoral intern, Bill as my clinical supervisor.

Bill asked me during my interview for the internship if I frequented campus bathrooms for sex; I did not...and told him so. Evidently, this had been an issue with other interns.

I was one of a group of out doctoral students — male and female — who taught — with Bill in the sociology department — a hugely well attended and wholly unprecedented undergraduate course on LGBTQ sexuality. Our guest lecturers were a who's who of the leadership of the then still-nascent post-Stonewall gay community in the San Francisco Bay Area. The course had a refreshingly defiant and celebratory tone. I participated as a graduate teaching assistant in the first two years it was offered. The class's celebratory tone was well deserved.

It was exhilarating to be out to that extent — and I understood well that there was no turning back to one foot — or even both feet — in the closet.

Sadly, during this same time, a darkness was emerging in the LGBTQ community — one that soon none of us could ignore. The encroaching AIDS epidemic was breaking into public awareness. It was known initially — in New York — as GRID, gay-related immune deficiency.

I had known Gary Walsh years prior — as Nick's roommate in the apartment they shared near Dolores Park — just down the hill from the home that Tim, Tom-dog, and I shared at a different time. In May 1983, Gary — a psychotherapist working in the gay community — was a person with AIDS (PWA) and lead organizer of the first San Francisco AIDS Memorial Candlelight March. Gary and I spoke warmly after the march concluded. He died in February of the following year at age thirty-nine.

He was the first of many I had known or would come to know who were infected and eventually died. From this time forward, AIDS was woven inextricably into the fabric of all of our lives.

I paid the bills initially, at Berkeley, by tending bar at the Bench and Bar, a gay bar in Oakland — while attempting to get on staff as a waiter at Chez Panisse in Berkeley. The

Bench and Bar is where I met stunningly dark-featured, handsome, endearingly shy, and alluringly seductive bad-boy Michael; we became not quite boyfriends but definitely friends who happened to have an occasional and complicated sexual relationship. He worked as a department store designer/decorator — from the street-facing display windows to the floor-by-floor seasonal/thematic displays du jour throughout the store. I worked for and with him one holiday season. It was fun and fascinating — a whole world I knew nothing about. Michael was a very talented guy — and one of my first photography models, a then-nascent passion that endured for many years.

I was eventually hired and started waiting in the upstairs café at Chez Panisse...until Alice Waters saw me on the floor one day. She had not personally authorized my hiring; I had been hired without consultation by one of her minor partners, the very sweet Tom Guernsey — evidently a no-no.

The lovely late Helen Gustafson was a hostess there at the time and came to my rescue by introducing me to Laurence DeVries, then general manager and sommelier at the nearby Santa Fe Bar and Grill — where an emerging superstar chef named Jeremiah Tower — who had earlier cooked with Alice at Chez Panisse — was drawing international attention for the brilliance and creativity of his "California cuisine," which many would say he led in putting on the culinary map.

I was at the café long enough to meet and establish a sexual friendship with one of the pastry chefs — who later died of AIDS.

I worked with Laurence — who became a personal friend — and Jeremiah and his amazing crew for the rest of my time studying at Berkeley — which prompted one of my professors to lament one day, "I wish more of our students worked at something interesting like that."

The kitchen crew were all professionals at the top of their game, several of them stars in their own right. The front of the house — bartenders, waiters, busboys — were often students — many at Berkeley. Edward, my favorite bartender, was a law student; Fawn, one of my favorite waiter colleagues, was a lay graduate student at the Graduate Theological Union; Warren, another favorite, was completing an undergraduate degree; Siggy was studying design; Donna, a hostess, went on to complete her own doctorate at Yale. A couple of the guys also became models for me. Jeremiah, Laurence, and several others on staff were openly gay.

We worked hard — all with a deep respect for Jeremiah — learned an enormous amount about food and wine...and had a total blast!

Jeremiah opened his San Francisco extravaganza — STARS — when I was close to finishing my studies; I was one of the opening waiters, but returned to the SFBG to assist Warren, who had become the manager when all the heavy hitters moved across the bay to staff STARS.

People whose names I had only known from wine labels — like Mondavi, Phelps, and Neyers — routinely popped in with a new wine they wanted Jeremiah — and the waitstaff — to taste. We were often invited to visit them at their wineries. I particularly treasure the memory of a luncheon with a small group of other waiters, hosted by Robert and Margrit Mondavi at their winery in Oakville, and a small luncheon at the Neyers residence in St. Helena in honor of Laurence's birthday — for which Bruce retired to their cellar to select a wine vinted in Laurence's birth year.

Looking back, I'd have to say that I — by and large — liked and enjoyed my restaurant colleagues much more than I did my psychology colleagues later on. They were more authentic and present — fun and spontaneous, creative, and generous of spirit.

By comparison — and likely also describing myself — I found psychologists often to be overdeveloped intellectually and underdeveloped both emotionally and psychologically. We/they have a tendency to wield our diagnostic training as both a shield and a weapon, ensuring distance. I found working closely with other psychologists in an academic setting "interesting," and supervising them as a group an ongoing challenge — a tough herding of cats. There is no scarier human gathering than a national conference of psychologists.

I resumed my drives through and visits to Big Sur — taking breaks from school, driving south to visit Sharon and/or my parents. As with other moments previously mentioned, time spent in Big Sur during this period was profoundly mean- ingful. I suppose, in ways, this magical coast took the place of what a physical church might have been to me as a child — a place of wonder, renewal, solace, prayer, and sanctuary. It fed my soul and was always there for me, never disappointing.

Close friends at the time, who knew my family history, asked me why I continued to visit my parents — and espe- cially my father after my mother died. My reply was simply that the more I was able to resolve with him, internally, while he was alive, the freer I would be from him after his death. I think today that I made the right decision.

Sharon and her husband had become major pot farmers on the central coast during my earlier years at Berkeley, before their baby was born. One weekend, when I drove down for a visit, unwittingly at harvest time, I was requisitioned to join a team trimming the leaves away from the more desirable buds to ready the crop for market — which in this case meant some bands in LA. I was sent home with welcome cash and a grocery bag about half full of the otherwise-to-be-discarded leaves — an absolute bonanza for me. My friends back home and I feasted accordingly.

Sharon took flying lessons during this time, but did not complete requirements for a license; the thinking was that it would facilitate transport of their product to market. A bit later, after a few very successful crops, they branched out into dealing cocaine — with a dramatically different, mean, and sometimes violent clientele — a forebodingly irresistible temptation for Sharon.

So in my public life post-London, I was a waiter, student, and — eventually — fledgling psychotherapist and junior professor. In my private life, I was also, as mentioned, a photographer — with portraits and art studies of comely young men as my subject of choice.

My first model was a former ASL student who stayed a few days with me in Berkeley during the time that I was a graduate student; he was an undergraduate at a different university nearby and volunteered to model for me. There have been scores of models since, shot in locations in several parts of the world — often during interludes at professional meetings/conferences I was attending, which I almost always found tedious, filled with hot air, and a waste of time and money.

My one stint as a wedding photographer was for a favorite model, George; my zero-dollar rates were the best he could afford. His bride and their families did not complain. Later, I was hugely flattered when the twin sons of an art-college colleague in Colorado asked me to take their high school graduation photos.

Several personal friends have long been familiar with my photography; I had a show in San Francisco in 1992, and have entered a couple of individual photos in exhibitions, but have mostly simply collected images — which now number into the thousands.

The 2023 film *Luther: The Fallen Sun* presents the powerful assumption that our secret lives house our shame, which is so powerful that we will do almost anything to avoid exposure.

Simultaneous with my public and private lives, in my secret life — which was definitely where I parked my shame, terrified that others could see what lie therein — I was hiring male escorts/hustlers for sexual companionship. My first, mentioned earlier, was in the early 1970s while living with Nick on Holyoke Street in San Francisco; there was then a several-year lapse before a series of young adult men accompanied me, on and off in this way, throughout the better part of my graduate study for a decade or so. This practice then, interestingly, ceased altogether once I completed both graduate degrees.

I typically picked up guys who were "working the street" on Polk Street in San Francisco; usually we went back to my place in Berkeley or Oakland. The Jungian analyst I was working with at the time in my own psychotherapy described this activity as an overt attempt to retrieve/regain/reconnect with parts of my lost youth — with guys who for the most part had themselves been abandoned, abused, and cast out — sometimes living on the streets. On some level, we shared a bond whose glue was private shame and distorted sexuality.

I visited one guy, Aaron, in San Quentin, where he was doing a stint for I don't remember what. He asked for some toiletries and personal items. Another guy had just gotten out of the army; another maintained a very tidy and tasteful apartment where he received his "guests" with a certain grace. Often appearing quite hardened, these guys could also be tender, funny, and kind.

Looking back, I see that I was somehow able unconsciously to recreate the very dynamic that I grew up with: publicly, the A student and happy-go-lucky minor athlete; privately and secretly, a participant in a tormented and twisted, highly sexualized, guilt-ridden dance...all wrapped in secret shame.

In round two, however, I believe now that I was individuating — bringing to the surface and into my awareness — the particulars of this dynamic with a view to better understanding it, gaining control over it, and ultimately begin integrating the split-off parts of myself that it represented.

The parallels between the gravitational center of my father's secret life — young boys — and that of my own — young men — isn't lost on me. Perhaps hidden in the murky depths of his pathology, the roots of his evil compulsion to steal the innocence of others reflected some trauma of his own, whereby his own innocence was stolen. I'll now never know with absolute certainty, but I didn't unearth a shred of evidence of this being the case. At the same time, it's no mystery to me why and how I so identified with young men who were sex workers and living on the margins of society. Both Jung's concept of infection of the psyche and my own later work conceptualizing the imprinted arousal pattern (IAP) come to mind in this context. I'll talk about both later in the book.

Looking back, I am fascinated by the realization that my graduate studies and my dalliance with escorts ran essentially parallel; I seem to have graduated from both at about the same time.

I would also — during my time at Berkeley — occasionally again visit gay bathhouses — once with a roommate, but usually on my own. I ran into Gregory during one visit, and a work colleague of Michael's on another. In Berkeley for a brief period, I dated a young guy, Paul, who worked at the Steam Works baths there. Where the Barracks in San Francsico had been my then-shocking and eye-opening introduction to gay bathhouses, this was now a decade later, and I had developed a comfort with these venues.

It was still the early to mid-1980s. AIDS was a percolating predator as we patrons engaged in all manner of anonymous sex. There were orgy rooms and steam rooms and private rooms — all dimly lit. The bathhouses were a shadowy and anonymous opportunity for collective connection and release in wild abandon — aspects of our post-Stonewall sexual liberation — hence, in part, ironically celebratory.

The virus could hardly have had a more ideal environment for its spread; those of us who partook but emerged unscathed were very fortunate.

As I progressed through my graduate studies, with surreal timing and dark choreography, somewhere from the depths, my family — in the persons of my father, brother, and sister — inserted itself in deeply unconscious ways that felt like an undertow, a powerful current seeking to hold me in place even as I inched increasingly toward the freedom of a potentially shamelessly integrated public and private life.

Both my father and brother had major health crises during the time of my graduate study — impossible to ignore and a huge suck on my spiritual and psychological energies. Sharon, who had been bullied by her husband into aborting two or three prior pregnancies, secretly sought my counsel when she again became pregnant. She was in part concerned that she would not succeed at raising a child. Assuring her that I would always take and never abandon any child of hers — and mourning with her the ones that neither of us ever got the chance to know — Sharon decided not to abort this time and gave birth ten weeks prematurely, smack-dab in the middle of my orals exam preparation.

Albeit far more powerful, in no way consciously intentional, and deeply rooted, this felt like the family's version of Suzanne's and Hans's earlier admonitions; all seemed to sense, as I did, that staying the course I had charted for myself and seeing it to completion would deliver me into a new and different reality from the one I had left behind. The family "undertow" in particular makes me think today of the dynamic in which, for example, a battered spouse will stay with her/his abuser — even when they could have escaped. Something in the relational dynamic seeks mightily to maintain control — and I'd suggest that the roots of that "something" may well be generational. I definitely felt both the undertow and my own determination to individuate against its pull.

Others let me know — directly and indirectly — that they perceived my stubborn insistence on moving forward as selfish — and not fair to them.

My niece, Leia, arrived — as noted above — a tad early, in July 1983. I learned of her birth via a message from Sharon — "Guess what? You're an uncle." — on my answering machine. The baby was medevacked from Morro Bay, where Sharon had delivered her unexpectedly at our father's house, to the intensive-care nursery (ICN) at San Francisco General Hospital, weighing in at two pounds, ten ounces.

I picked Sharon up at the airport the next day, and we went immediately to see the new arrival. She was, of course, tiny and spread out under a heat lamp — all manner of tubes and wires connected to her, as they had been to her grandmother just before her departure five years earlier. I touched her little hand, and she wrapped her doll-like tiny fingers around my index finger and squeezed. I was all in from that moment forward.

Sharon moved in with me; I was living in a small studio apartment near Lake Merritt at the time, diligently preparing for my doctoral orals. We made the trip across the bay to be with Leia at least daily. The more we got to know Leia and her fellow premies, the more full-term babies looked gigantic to us.

In the evenings at the ICN, we got to know the attendant nurses well. The physicians, by and large, had gone home for the day by that time and were on call as needed. These wonderful, loving women — I don't recall there being any men amongst them — taught us a great deal about the premie reality — beyond diagnosis and the chart at the end of the bed. Also — typically, we learned — the babies' fathers stayed away.

Phil Cowan (member of my dissertation committee) and his lovely wife, Carolyn, had had a premie a generation earlier — at which time they were not allowed tactile interaction and could only look at their baby through glass from the corridor. We bonded — and commiserated — over these similar but different events in our lives.

We'll meet adult Leia later in this telling; she's alive and well and quite the character as I write today.

I completed and handed in my dissertation in 1985. At that time, the clerk who received and logged in your dissertation handed you a piece of hard candy — a kind of ritual recognition that you had walked in the door with the product of several years' labor in your hand — and then would have left empty-handed, but for the candy. I got it immediately when I walked out the door — a gigantic weight lifted, a tiny sweet reward in its place.

As part of my academic program, one completed an MA en route to their PhD. I completed my MA in 1983 — the year my niece was born — after which I was eligible to begin seeing private clients as a psychological assistant working under the supervision of a licensed psychologist. This allowed me to begin building my private practice.

Completing my doctorate allowed me to begin the post-doctoral portion of the required 3,000 supervised hours as a condition of eligibility to sit for the two-step licensure process to become a psychologist: a national written exam, followed by a state oral exam. It took me a couple of attempts to pass the written exam (my lack of undergraduate psychology studies took its toll), but I became independently licensed as a California psychologist in 1988 at age forty-one.

Ken — a different Ken, not my older brother — was seeing one of my colleagues in our private-practice offices on Channing Way in Berkeley; our eyes met in the waiting room, as he was waiting for his appointment and I was getting some cold water from the refrigerator, between clients. Fast-forward, and we're living together as a couple in the Rockridge area of Oakland — where I'm writing my dissertation, and he is completing his master of social work (MSW) at Berkeley. We were excellent companions during this time of shared academic pursuit; Ken once credited our being in a relationship at this time — roughly 1984–1986 — as one of the reasons neither of us contracted AIDS — which was then spreading throughout the gay community like wildfire — before most of us realized it. He was certainly not wrong about that.

My father, Jeremiah Tower, and Bill Merriweather hung out together in one corner of our kitchen in that Oakland flat during my PhD graduation party in 1985. My doctoral robe hung against the door leading into the living room. It was a full house and a hugely complimentary cast of characters, which included Nick, his mother, and mutual friends from the Grass Valley area, including our old neighbors from Holyoke Street; Fawn, Edward, and others from the restaurant; Berkeley classmates; and mutual friends of Ken's and mine. Sharon did not attend; in fairness, she had a two-year-old at home.

It was a great party!

Section Three

Adulting — Laying Claim

Finally, we visit life on the "other side" — still a work in progress as I approach eighty, but light-years improved over the early years.

Part IV

Healer, Heal Thyself

Chapter Twelve
Private Practice and AIDS

"AIDS and age have taken their toll," intoned the woman standing next to our previously nearly impossible-to-get center-front seats in the orchestra section of San Francisco Opera House, where my friend and fellow psychologist George and I had season tickets for the San Francisco Ballet. She explained to us that the customary occupants of this section had long been like family — the same folk, always happy to see one another — season after season. Some had succumbed to their advancing years, others to AIDS. George and I were the beneficiaries, showing up as new and unfamiliar faces, who were met — not in an unfriendly manner — by the lamentations of the woman who wistfully noted the transition.

AIDS and the beginning years of my fourteen-year psychotherapy practice (1983–1997) intersected; my practice was heavily impacted by the epidemic — something for which my formal training had in no way prepared me.

Less than two decades after the jubilation of the Stonewall Riots — signaling gay "liberation" from societal oppression — the AIDS epidemic consumed the gay community in a crushing and inescapable wave of trauma. In those first seemingly interminable years, the virus was a death sentence, a killer of thousands that terrified the entire community internationally. We were a community in shock.

For me, just as I was beginning to emerge from the long shadow of my personal trauma and to experience life for the first time as a more consciously integrated person, my personal and professional lives became intertwined with the epidemic.

Summer 1985, just after completing my PhD, Sharon, Roy, toddler Leia, and I traveled east — as referenced earlier, first to Iowa to celebrate Roy's mother's ninetieth birthday, and then on to Cape Cod, staying with Mac and Jeanne to celebrate Ellen's mother's eightieth birthday (Ellen had died in late 1978). This was the last time I would see my father's parents and the last, save one, that I would see my mother's mother.

After that trip — AIDS having exploded in the San Francisco Bay Area — the need for mental health professionals expanded exponentially with the epidemic. I was amongst the first group in a special training conducted by the AIDS Health Project — housed at UC San Francisco and led by Dr. Jim Dilley. We were trained to facilitate support groups for the newly seroconverted, for the worried well, and for those who were unwilling or unable to stop engaging in high-risk sexual behaviors.

Hal Dillehunt was a psychologist PWA who also participated in the training whilst serving as clinical director of the Shanti Project — which provided a huge range of essential services for the HIV community, led by Jim Geary. Hal and I became friends of sorts. He had a beautiful home just outside of the Castro neighborhood in San Francisco, wherein, he once lamented, he had hoped to "seduce half of San Francisco."

As his illness progressed, Hal wanted to make one last trip to Europe while still able, and asked me to fill in for him at Shanti, which I agreed to do — taking leave of my restaurant career at the same time. When Hal returned (briefly) to Shanti, Jim Geary asked me to cover for some other supervisory case managers as they became too ill to continue in their jobs, which I also agreed to do.

Mid-December 1990, between clients, I picked up a home voicemail from my office in Berkeley. Sharon's voice, in a matter-of-fact way, said, "Guess what? Dad died." She had learned the news from a teenage boy who had been living at the house and found our father's body. I had just enough time before my next client to call her back, my own shock mirroring hers, and agree that I'd meet her in Morro Bay the next day.

The song "Ding-Dong! The Witch is Dead" running on continuous loop in the back of my mind, I returned to that day's remaining clients — one of my more difficult moments of challenge to the therapist's responsibility to be ever-present for the client and hold one's own "stuff" apart and away from the clinical interaction.

After meeting my last client, I drove home, calling Ken from my car. I agreed to meet his plane from Seattle the next morning in San Luis Obispo and go together to the house — Roy's body had been removed — before Sharon arrived after driving up from San Diego. I informed clients scheduled for the rest of that week that I would need to cancel our meetings due to a family emergency, knowing that there would be a range of reactions — and non-reactions — when I returned.

On my drive south the next day, I called Roy's brothers — he was the first of them to die — and Uncle Mac to let them know that Roy had passed away. While waiting for Ken's plane to arrive, I called the mortuary to arrange for us to view the body before it was cremated.

When we arrived at the house, Ken — who had been named executor of the estate — went immediately into Roy's bedroom and closed the door. Exactly what he was looking for or expected to find, I'll never know. We learned later that he had Roy's mail forwarded to his address and would allow no one else to collect the mail at home.

Some years earlier, after an unusual and infrequent dinner together in San Francisco, standing just the two of us on a street corner before returning to our cars, I looked my brother in the eye and said, "Dad molested me as a boy — he did you too, didn't he?" He gave me a stunned look, said nothing, and turned and walked away.

Like our father, my brother spent over twenty years in the US Navy — his time mostly in intelligence and nuclear submarines — and retired at the same rank as our father, lieutenant commander.

In another of our rare times alone together, when Ken was still in the navy and stationed in San Diego, we were driving to Sharon's house when he suddenly blurted out — in a highly agitated tone of voice — that the police had come to his apartment, demanding entry. Ken said he initially refused, then relented, and was told that there had been a 911 call from his apartment — evidently made by a young man who was not present when the police arrived. My guess then and now is that there had been a young man in his apartment, that he had felt unsafe and had called 911…and that Ken allowed him to flee before the police arrived.

What secrets my brother took with him — his own and any he may have shared with our father — we will never know. My gut tells me that's just as well.

Numb and on autopilot at our father's home, I set to work cleaning the pool of dried blood in the corner of the dining area where Roy had fallen and died — from an esophageal hemorrhage caused by his acute alcoholism — not wanting Sharon to see it.

The boy who had called Sharon came by the house shortly after we three siblings had all arrived. None of us had ever seen or met him. He too was in shock. He asked to collect his belongings and let us know where we could find Roy's wallet and other personal effects. We gave him a love note addressed to him that we found in Roy's bedroom. I then gently asked him to leave the three of us alone. Roy's last boy-friend — no one knows how many there were.

Sharon and I went to view the body and, later, to collect Roy's ashes. Ken stayed at the house. At the mortuary, Roy's remains were laid out under a white sheet, his many-years-of-consuming-great-quantities-of-alcohol distended belly a notable protuberance. His face was frozen in a scowl, likely his autonomic response to the shock of sour bile that would have accompanied his hemorrhage. I lightly stroked his beard as we turned to take our leave.

We agreed to inform Fred — by now in his midtwenties and living with a girlfriend — of Roy's death and to invite him to join us in spreading Roy's ashes. Our own feelings about the Roy-Fred relationship notwithstanding, we knew that it had been an important one to both of them, each in his own way. I drove over to Fred's video store — which he had purchased from Roy — found him there alone, and delivered the news. He too was shocked and agreed right away that he wanted to join the three of us the next morning to spread Roy's ashes.

Roy's house was only a few blocks up the hill from the beach, so we all walked down together. It was a clear and sunny, but biting-cold, December morning. Pressed against my body, I carried the cardboard box containing the ashes — a final embrace, one of the few we ever had. We agreed on a spot along the beach, a bit north of where the road ended.

I surprised myself — and Sharon — that I wept as our tiny procession made its way along the sand toward the spot we had chosen. He had been my father, after all; I wept for what was...and what was not.

I opened the box and, before cutting open the plastic bag within that held the ashes, asked if anyone wanted to say anything. Ken remonstrated that Roy had directed that there be no service; I replied that I thought a few words would be OK. With the exception of Ken, each of us said a few words of farewell.

I cut open the bag and tipped the contents such that they ran through my fingers into the sea — mostly fine ash, bits of more solid stuff, likely bone. I shook out the bag so all its contents would fall into the water, and that was that. We processed in silence back to the house; Fred took his leave, and I don't believe that any of us ever saw him again. It was as if we four had shed a shared skin, finally freed from it, liberated in ways we had not known possible — the shedding carrying different meaning for each of us.

We three siblings spent much of the day's remainder sorting through and emptying out the house — taking what little we wanted for ourselves, conveying piles of clothing to Goodwill. Ken spoke with the probate attorney. We had most recently been together — with Roy — only the month before, at Ken's retirement ceremony from the US Navy in San Diego. There was a lightness to our final evening together. We went out to dinner, were relaxed with one another, told stories, laughed, and planned our departures for the next day.

The next and final time we'd be together would be a mere fifteen months later, in March 1992, as Sharon and I stood with Ken's widow and stepson at the mortuary in Washington state, having asked to view Ken's body together before his own cremation.

Michael was one of my closest friends to contract AIDS. I was one of the small group of family and friends who stayed with him 24/7 at the end of his life in order to allow him to die at home. Together with his mother, I was with him at the end. Before the coroner came to remove his body, she asked if I could retrieve a favorite ring of his and give it to her, which I did — one last intimate moment together, Michael's beloved black cat watching me, circling on the bed next to his body.

Michael's mom and I watched together from an upstairs balcony as two attendants loaded the body bag containing his remains into their large station-wagon-type vehicle. She sighed; we both wept a bit; there was both sadness and relief in the finality.

Michael took up abstract painting when he became too ill to work or spend time independently outside his apartment near Lake Merrit in Oakland. He gave a painting to each of us who were with him for the final period of his young life; he was thirty-seven when he died. Mine hangs in my study here at home today.

Michael did not have an easy early life. He was abandoned early in life by his father; his mother raised him and his younger brother alone. He was sexually abused as a boy. Moments of trust were rare and precious for him.

Michael's and Ken's dying intersected — Michael's playing out more slowly, the outcome never in doubt; Ken's more abrupt, coming as something of a surprise, even though we all knew that his drinking was heavy and constant. Evidently, it intensified after Roy's passing; Sharon and I later learned that he was drunk pretty much day and night in his final months.

By the time Ken was hospitalized, it was too late — he had essentially pickled all his vital organs. The extent of the damage perhaps not yet clear to his physician, Sharon and I were encouraged to stay away during his initial hospitalization, the thought being that our presence would somehow complicate his then still-hoped-for recovery. Meanwhile, we were told later, a hospital volunteer sat by his bed and read to him, which he was said to enjoy.

It took the arrival home from Austria of his stepson, Jonathan, and his assessment of the situation, to alert us that Ken's death was imminent. Sharon and I jumped on the first flights we could — she from San Diego and I from San Francisco. My flight arrived first; I called the hospital for an update and was told that my older brother had passed. When Sharon stepped off her flight, I had to tell her that we were too late. Ken had died from cerebral edema — his formidable brain had swollen beyond his skull's capacity to contain it — he was forty-seven years old.

We spent a day or two with Ken's widow and stepson. We went together to view his body. He had an amazing look of peace on his face — one none of us could remember seeing for years. Eerily, laid out on the mortuary table, his body, too, had the telltale protuberance that Roy's had had. The old saying "Like father, like son" had taken on a new dimension.

Outside the mortuary, in the moments afterwards, we all walked off in different directions in silence, alone with the moment. The next day, we four went back to the hospital together and asked to meet with Ken's attending physician. We chastised him for telling us to stay away, letting him know that he had robbed us all of a chance to say goodbye — and asked him to remember Ken and his family going forward, as he advised other families in similar circumstances.

Sharon and I took a couple of walks together in Ken's neighborhood. On one, we passed an antique store, which was closed. Looking in the display window, I saw a bronze statue of Mercury, messenger of the gods, that spoke to me. It turned out to be a Giovanni da Bologna reproduction, the original from the seventeenth century. It was a team effort procuring and storing it so that I could collect it when

I returned to collect Ken's ashes months later. Today, it graces our bedroom dresser — a reminder both of Ken and the fact that one simply never knows what the gods might have in store for us.

Michael was angry with me when I got back to Oakland after Ken's death. He was unsympathetic to my brother's passing — perhaps because it foreshadowed his own, I'm not sure. But he was clear that he wanted me there, with the others, for the duration.

Ken's passing hit me harder and more deeply than either of my parents' deaths had — he was my older brother; we shared a bedroom as children; we grew up together. I can't say we were ever close as kids, but I had hopes that we could change that as adults. We were both molested by the same father, the one who had at one point wistfully admitted that "Ken got the worst of it." Later, when I had the time and opportunity, in a solitary memorial for Ken, I drove the sacred-to-me and ever-available-sanctuary coast along Big Sur, stopped at a favorite and somewhat-isolated overlook, and played Mozart's "Requiem" on my car's sound system — over and over — while gazing numbly out over the sea.

AIDS by then had cut a wide and deep swath through the gay and the larger communities. There were so many so quickly that I started to keep a list of people who had somehow entered and touched my life, personally and professionally, who also had HIV — my AIDS Angels. There were over a hundred names on my list, more than half of people who had died. I know well that many in our community, particularly caregivers and longtime survivors living with HIV, counted far greater numbers on whatever kind of list they maintained for themselves.

The names on my list included several former clients; Michael's former lover and Michael himself; my former physician; my former therapist; a former graduate professor; restaurant friends from my table-waiting, graduate-school days; colleagues from AIDS trainings, agencies, and symposia (including Hal); a couple of former boyfriends, including Gregory.

Siggy was on my list. He was a remarkable soul in so many ways: the first Black firefighter In Orange County, California; designer extraordinaire, he designed the restroom interiors at STARS, where we both worked as waiters. He was one of the funniest and most joyfully irreverent people I have ever known. As with Michael, a circle of family and friends stayed with Siggy 24/7 in his final days. His father, a retired Marine, was amongst them. I took him one day to STARS for lunch and to show him his son's design work; he was duly impressed. After Siggy died, his circle was offered items from his apartment — across from Dolores Park — to remember him by. I chose a painting that had hung in his bathroom, which hangs in our hallway today. An abstract, it's a cluster of white circles and spheres against a black background, with a solitary red square positioned amongst them in the lower right. I've always seen the red square as Siggy — distinctive, amongst and apart at the same time. For his memorial, we chartered a boat to spread his ashes in San Francisco Bay.

Siggy and Hal never met, but I inherited from Hal the facilitation of a therapy group for a religious community a block from Siggy's apartment. I often went from one to the other.

We all tested anxiously for the virus; almost none of us could be certain that we had not been exposed and infected. I tested several times. Fortuitously, I tested negative each time.

I began to get more and more referrals to my private practice from men (the epidemic, of course, also impacted women, but few showed up in my practice) who were somewhere along the HIV continuum — from worried but well...to at risk...to newly seroconverted...to symptomatic...to seriously ill...to dying. These clients populated my clinical calendar alongside continuing referrals of graduate and undergraduate students from the university...presenting with a complex array of issues — from anxiety to depression, to writer's block, to sexual identity, to couple and family matters.

A close colleague, social psychologist Dr. Greg Herek, asked me to write the lead chapter for his 1995 book *AIDS, Identity, and Community: The HIV Epidemic and Lesbians and Gay Men, Psychological Perspectives on Lesbian Gay Issues*, which was published by Division 44 of the American Psychological Association. My chapter, "HIV and the Gay Male Community: One Clinician's Reflections over the Years," became the framing narrative for the otherwise-empirical studies that were the focus of the volume. In this chapter — beyond what seems relevant to this particular tale — I describe the complex interplay of personal and professional issues, the living and dying, and the fear and hope that characterized my experience as a clinician during those very traumatic years. I discuss the experience of several clients, friends, and associates as they battled the HIV virus — a losing battle for many. An excerpt from this chapter follows here.

With one particular long-term client, Bill, who was both severely paranoid and addicted to anonymous sexual activity, and had little success with satisfactory human connection in his life, this move away from traditional psychotherapeutic practice was particularly pronounced. When Bill began to develop dementia, and became too disoriented to drive or travel by public transportation, we would meet weekly in his apartment. Once the dementia progressed and he was no longer able to care for himself at home, our meetings took place at an AIDS hospice where Bill was then in residence. When he was hospitalized with his second bout of PCP, we met in his hospital room. He died while a resident in a second hospice, in a blissful dementia oblivious to the painful and solitary reality he had known as an adult.

I'll never forget our last visit, the most endearing of all the years we had worked together. Bill had melted into an uncharacteristically relaxed comfort with the other residents and staff, and had become able to accept and delight in the affectionate attention he received from them. He finally had the long elusive experience of belonging here in the AIDS hospice. When I last saw him, we sat in the rear garden and Bill wore a straw bonnet with a red ribbon and asked me if I liked it. I did and told him so. He asked me if the Rolls was parked in front as he had instructed; I said I hadn't seen it on the way in. With a beneficent and imperial wave of his hand, he said, "Oh, the staff must be using it again; I told them it was okay." On my way out that day, the staff person at the desk remarked that I was one of only two people who came to see Bill. The other, a man I had never met, called me a week later to tell me that Bill had died. I like to think that Bill's and my success at connecting during our long clinical relationship before and during his illness somehow facilitated his bittersweet experience of family at the end of his life.

Worth saying again, but differently: little did I realize, when I left ASL in 1980 — as a high school guidance counselor with a BA in English — to begin graduate studies, how transformative and literally lifesaving this period of time would be. This phase of my life was like a tunnel which I entered at one end as one person and exited at the other a very different person.

In my public life, I completed my doctorate while waiting tables, satisfying pre- and postdoctoral internship requirements, and beginning my own psychotherapy practice. In my private life, I undertook a variety of my own therapies and launched into my personal photography with male models.

In my secret life, I was frequenting male escorts.

I worked as a client with a half-dozen therapists during these formative years — male and female, traditional psychotherapists as well as Jungian analysts, and one hypnotherapist. The aggregate benefit to both my acuity as a therapist — and, of course, intimately related, my own personal/psychological/ spiritual growth, health, and awareness — was enormous.

I learned the importance of doing one's own deep work as a therapist and the dangers of working in the lives of others when one had not. One of my first therapists — when I was a graduate student working as a waiter at the Santa Fe Bar and Grill in Berkeley — showed up, clearly inebriated, with his partner, at the restaurant and asked for my section. I was stunned and dismayed at this atrocious judgment and utter lack of boundaries. I fired him in one last session, wherein he seemed puzzled at my reaction and said he thought of their visit as a compliment and that it was cool to have a client working at such a celebrated restaurant.

Albeit unneeded, this was yet another reminder, early in my own formation as a therapist, of how damaging such a lack of boundaries — especially in a power-differential relationship — can be…and a huge lesson in the necessity of setting and keeping appropriate boundaries.

Chapter Thirteen
Individuation

All three aspects of my life — public, private, and secret — of course, ran on parallel frequencies, simultaneously. What I had to have known intuitively — a much-undervalued form of intelligence, in my opinion — was that the intertwining of the three moved me into a more conscious integration of formerly scattered and fragmented aspects of myself; in Jung's terms, I was continuing to individuate — taking a huge leap in becoming the unique and once-in-time expression of the universal soul that happens to be me.

I had consciously abandoned the Christian notion of perfection — casting out the dark and the "sinful" in pursuit of being Christlike — in favor of seeking a more humble and realistic goal of wholeness — integrating the shadow, embracing my always-to-be-with-me task of becoming more conscious, more aware, more whole — a never-ending process in which the notion of perfection is irrelevant.

And, finally, I was no longer flailing — I had tools and knowledge and understandings that — though they by no means erased the trauma and chaos of my early life — gave me a heretofore inconceivable sense of the possibility of being at the helm — having control of my life — and choosing where to steer and where not to.

It was Carl Rogers who observed that one can be at once a therapist, imperfect, and helpful to others. I remember being hugely relieved at this dictum.

My psychotherapy practice was, without question, the most humbling, impactful, and gratifying of all my professional endeavors over the years. I came to see it as a spiritual practice in which my clients and I crafted and engaged together in a sacred space that often — but not always — wrought healing and positive change in both the lives of my clients and, to be perfectly honest, my own. To be entrusted with another person's psyche, vulnerabilities, fears, wounds, and hopes is a gigantic honor…and responsibility. I am in awe today when thinking back on the uniquely private and alchemical environment that many clients and I created for our work.

Often new clients arrived embarrassed or feeling stigmatized, as if something must be wrong with them if they needed "help." I learned, on the contrary — both from my own experience and from observing my clients — that choosing to enter into psychotherapy was an act of courage, hope, and strength. I told my clients that they were brave and strong.

Participants were electing to improve their quality of life overall, including their mental and spiritual well-being. They wanted to feel better, understand more deeply, and enjoy more fulfilling relationships — intimate, professional, and casual. Invariably, I came to deeply respect and feel a new kind of love for each client as s/he engaged in their unique process of healing.

Clients also came to experience the "space" we created together as a world apart. One saw me eating my lunch at a café near my office one day, and later confessed that it had never occurred to him that I existed outside the office. Another, after a chance encounter in the lobby of a local movie theater, simply stood frozen in place, jaw fallen open.

Some of the work — and its outcomes — were relatively superficial and less impactful — for which there were a number of explanatory variables: we weren't the right fit; the presenting issues were relatively minor and easily addressed; the tenderness of what needed addressing was too great — one could barely touch it, let alone fully engage it.

It wasn't long before I recognized that the experience of trauma — mild to horrific — was the common thread running through the lives of most — if not all — of my clients. In that sense, my own trauma — and the empathy for others that it allowed, not in the least abstract — became an invaluable asset in my practice as a psychotherapist.

Much of the work was deeply transformative. Through my years-long efforts to engage my own healing, I was able to be an agent of healing for others — which in turn continued to deepen my own healing. I was able — both as a person and in the role of therapist — to stand in for those who had neglected or damaged my client(s) and facilitate a corrective experience, allowing the wounds and defenses from childhood to be gradually diminished, making room for spontaneity, optimism, growth, and possibilities heretofore unimagined — as adults.

Amongst those with whom this was the case was a young man who had never integrated the suicide of his older brother years earlier, and who, initially, shared his deep feelings of guilt (he blamed himself) and loss by leaving his journal for me to read between sessions. We eventually were able to engage his feelings face-to-face and enable him to live in loving memory of his brother in present time. Another was a biological female who tentatively revealed her transexual identity in describing a dream wherein she was a man in her sexual interactions. One very gentle man — whom I worked with almost all the time that I was in practice and who was the last client I saw when I closed it in 1997 — was so badly damaged by his early life that his longing for connection with others ran in equal depth to his anguish at fearing and sabotaging each opportunity that presented itself.

End-of-life issues in men far too young to be entertaining them became more and more of a focus. For several, I was the one who had to tell them that they could no longer work, or drive, or live alone — or were dying. We experienced and processed together the often-excruciating range of emotion that accompanied these stages of HIV/AIDS: denial, terror, rage, grief, despondency, sometimes acceptance.

In 1986, my father had lent me $5,000 to make a down payment on my first house in Rohnert Park, Sonoma County — even then, the closest to the Berkeley/San Francisco area that I could afford. Ken — my then partner — was clear that he was not going to be accompanying me on my move north, by which time our relationship had run its brief course; we did remain friends for several years afterwards. I celebrated my fortieth birthday in my new house, with a large and raucous party attended by a good cross section of friends from different parts of my life. My father was the only family member who attended.

Shortly thereafter, I began my five-year tenure as a lecturer in the Master's in Counseling program at Sonoma State University. I spent a good many hours at the campus library studying for my licensure exam, taking practice tests, etc. It took me three attempts to pass the national exam, my lack of undergraduate foundation in psychology meaning I had to pretty much teach myself what was needed for the exam.

I was nervous at first about teaching graduate students, but needn't have been — in this instance, it was a bit of a love affair, the relatively young, new PhD and his adult students, many contemporaries.

By 1988, I had passed both the written and oral exams for licensure as a psychologist in California and opened a second private-practice office in Santa Rosa, also Sonoma County.

That same year, Mike Lew published his pioneering work on male survivors of childhood sexual abuse, *Victims No Longer.* Mike's work facilitated both a new focus of my clinical work with adult victims of childhood sexual abuse, both male and female, as well as my own qualitative research focused on this population.

Also, after obtaining my own license, I joined with the gritty, community-based AIDS organizations that were providing services to the far-too-rapidly growing HIV population in Sonoma County. I was the only out psychologist in the county at the time. My new colleagues and I realized that there was a perilous lack of awareness and education in the frontline professional communities — including medical and law enforcement personnel — whose jobs required that they interact with this population. The stigma attached to LGBTQ folks, together with the terror of contracting HIV, often resulted in people being shunned, receiving hostile treatment, or being avoided by the persons and agencies they needed.

My Santa Rosa clientele was both similar and different from my Berkeley clientele. My referrals came from my community AIDS work, my increasing visibility with adult survivors of childhood sexual abuse, and the university.

One particularly memorable client was a nurse who had been abused as a child. In order to create sufficient safety for her to access and articulate her experience, we engineered a kind of adult playroom in my office. We set the sofa on its back; she would initially spend her time behind it, out-of-sight to me. She sometimes employed makeshift puppets to speak for her — an intermediate voice until the words needing to be spoken could find their way into her own. Sometimes there was silence from her side of the couch, interrupted by a sob, or an innocent little-girl voice asking innocent little-girl questions ("Why are you hurting me? What did I do wrong?"), or an angry-child voice remonstrating against her abuser. In time, we righted the couch and engaged face-to-face, adult to adult — with all of our behind-the-couch interactions now safe to reference together.

While at Sonoma State, I organized an on-campus regional conference on HIV/AIDS for all interested parties — lay and professional — who lacked the access to similar resources just an hour south in the San Francisco Bay Area. It was well attended.

For several years, beginning at Sonoma State, in my graduate child-development classes, I used my own experiences

— first-person — as a case study in describing the various impacts of child sexual abuse. One could always hear a pin drop during my presentation — which followed a reading and review of current literature in the field on this subject. Rich and poignant discussions, sometimes including other first-person tales from fellow survivors, always followed. One appreciative student, a mother of small children, indicated that she found my tale powerful and painful to hear and that it was clear to her that as a result of my early abuse, I was developmentally "stunted." It's an apt and very perceptive reaction that has stayed with me all these years since.

I became a full-time core faculty member at JFK University in the East Bay of the San Francisco Bay Area in 1992. I achieved the academic rank of professor there; my clinical practice continued, albeit with fewer clients. I closed my Sonoma County practice and worked exclusively out of my Berkeley office. I was asked by the dean of the Graduate School of Professional Psychology at JFK to take the lead in designing the university's first doctoral program, a professional "scientist practitioner" program, or PsyD — as opposed to the research-based PhD. The program admitted its first students in 1995; I was the founding program director.

The same year, I also bought my own Berkeley house — a very sweet, small, brown-shingle home built in 1906, on the west side of the UC campus.

Also in 1995, my book on male survivors, *Speaking Our Truth,* was published by Harper Collins in New York. I knew that this small book would never be either a bestseller or a coffee-table book, but felt that the then scant and still-emerging literature on male survivors lacked the voices of survivors themselves. So my contribution was an edited collection, focused on providing direct testimony, in the voices — and in one instance the artwork — of male survivors. I was particularly gratified to learn that the book had later been used in therapy groups for perpetrators, as an instrument in attempting to awaken empathy for their victims — to see and hear the effects of their actions.

Once the doctoral program at JFKU began to thrive, the university administration took it over. I started to feel that it was time for a new adventure. Toward the end of my tenure there, I played a leading role, together with a handful of colleagues who also worked with male survivors, in organizing a national conference focused on this population — which was held at JFKU the year after I left. I returned to facilitate and participate.

My clinical work continued to provide immediate raw and real material to incorporate into my graduate classes, whose students themselves were training to become psychotherapists. I of course spoke of my clients only in strict anonymity and only with clinically illustrative intent.

The focus/emphasis of my work life evolved over time. Initially, my private practice was essentially full time; then there was some adjunct teaching added in. In time, my teaching became full time, and my practice became part time. Then higher ed administration entered the picture, and the mix became part-time practice, part-time teaching, and part-time administration.

By the time I closed my practice in 1997, after fourteen years, I had become primarily an administrator who taught part time — and then, eventually and perhaps inevitably, a full-time administrator — my penance for the sins of my past lives.

My years as an administrator necessitated developing a thick skin, which seemed to evolve pretty naturally. After what I had survived as a child, there wasn't too much that was going to rattle me professionally.

My time in London and at ASL were seventeen years in the rearview mirror by the time I decided to close my practice and leave JFKU. My parents and older brother had died, as had so many of my AIDS Angels. It had been a remarkable journey. Professionally, there were notable successes, and I felt "adult" in ways I never had before. More importantly, personally, I had undertaken, directly parallel with my professional accomplishments and development, a deep investment in my own healing and mental and spiritual health. At the same time, I knew I wasn't "finished" and that this was a work I would need to continue to embrace throughout the remainder of my life. But, in a metaphorical sense, I could exhale for the first time.

People I had been close to before and even during my time in London — Nick, Hans, Suzanne, even Sharon — all noted that I had changed and was not the same person they had known previously. As I mentioned earlier, some felt — and even said — that I had somehow abandoned them in the process. I had become a different person — it's true — but I never wanted or intended to leave anyone else behind.

Chapter Fourteen
Finding Love – We Moved A Lot, V 2.0

I turned fifty in 1997, during my time living in Berkeley. While I had enjoyed a number of romantic and sexual relations over the years, none had actually stuck — and I assumed that I was simply too damaged to ever have the experience of a successful long-term partnership.

Then, very much by chance — and in an extremely narrow window of opportunity, against all odds — Peter and I met — online — in an AOL chat room. Still affected by the homophobia of his home environment, Peter was shyly exploring his sexuality after four years in the navy. He had moved to Northern California to work in the music industry and begin working on his undergraduate degree. He would turn twenty-eight later that year. We were both introverts preferring the anonymity of a digital meeting to the awkwardness of a face-to-face one — my earlier experience working in gay clubs notwithstanding.

Peter hadn't been in the chat room for long, and was about to leave — having been hit on by several men in uncomfortably aggressive sexual terms — when I entered, read his profile, and said simply hello. A friendly chat ensued, followed by an exchange of phone numbers, and a few phone calls. I invited him to dinner at the house in Berkeley. He accepted, though confessed later that he sat in his car for several minutes, looking at the front door, torn between driving off and knocking. He knocked; I answered.

Managed care had made private clinical practice less and less attractive, and my tenure at JFKU seemed to have run its course when I was offered an administrative faculty position in Phoenix, Arizona. So after a lot of conversation and consideration, Peter and I decided to move together. I sold the Berkeley house, we bought our first house together, and in many ways I fell in love with the desert Southwest, the horrific summer heat notwithstanding. Our move, in turn, drew Peter's then-newly divorced sister Martha there. We enjoyed a brief two years in residence — before being asked by the same organization to start up a new campus for them in Southern California. Martha stayed in Phoenix.

Love and Work

Sigmund Freud famously said, "Love and work are the cornerstones of our humanness." In other words, we become and get to know ourselves through our loves and our work.

As indicated earlier, work had been my addiction — and love an elusive mystery for much of my life. With a few lapses here and there, mostly during my bohemian period, I had worked from ages fifteen to seventy — for fifty-five years.

My work in restaurants was on and off, from the time I was fifteen to the time I finished graduate school at thirty-eight.

I washed dishes, tended bar, waited tables, cooked, and served as manager. I loved that business — learned a lot about food and wine…and life — and miss it. I met and worked side by side with many remarkable and talented people.

I worked in thirteen schools — five secondary and eight undergraduate and/or graduate — from ages twenty-one to sixty-seven. With the exception of my five years as a lecturer at Sonoma State University, all were small and private — both for and not-for-profit. None was Ivy League or top ten. I served as teacher/professor, counselor, administrator, and board member.

If I have one regret professionally, it's that I never had the opportunity to serve as president of a small, residential liberal-arts college…something that I always felt would be a great fit.

I spent fourteen years in private psychotherapy practice — from ages thirty-six to fifty — the longest I have worked at the same job ever. As I noted earlier, this was the most powerful, humbling, and rewarding work of my life.

I spent nearly a decade as a volunteer with the International Association of University Presidents (IAUP) — in leaderships roles — including president and chair of the board of directors — both inherited upon the untimely death of the gentleman who first invited me into a leadership role in his administration — Dr. J. Michael Adams. These roles (elaboration below) — which took me all over the world — overlapped with and extended beyond my last two university presidencies — concluding in Vienna, a few months after my seventieth birthday…and days before Sharon's death in summer 2017.

I threw myself into my work, and only well into retirement realized why not everyone did so. For most, work was a means to an end and — for the fortunate — an expression of self — which, together with family, formed the center of one's life — most frequently, not in that order. Work for me was the former and the latter since I had no family of my own to center me and absorb my energies...until I met Peter at age fifty.

I really didn't think that much about money and retirement as I moved along — pretty much just walking out one door when the time was right and through the next as opportunity allowed. I left a year's compensation on the table at one school (which I would have earned as a bonus after one more year of service) because the environment had become too hostile — and resigned, accepting a year's severance, shortly after signing a five-year contract worth over $2M at another for the same reason. I was and am a bit mystified by folks who can work at the same job and stay in the same place for decades — even though I realize they are likely in the majority.

Having embarked in 1997 on the most challenging new chapter of my life — where love AND work were intertwined — Peter and I moved nine times in seventeen years as my peripatetic career path took us here and there, and Peter (bless his good heart) started then interrupted several times his own academic and professional trajectories. We lived in four different states — California, Colorado (where Peter completed his bachelor's degree), Arizona, and New Hampshire (where Peter earned his master's degree, which I had the honor of conferring at commencement). We bought and sold ten homes during this time (1997–2014) — and rented three others along the way. Sharon once commented that "you guys just move around the country buying houses, fixing them up, then selling them and moving on to the next one." Peter and I discovered that we both enjoyed periodically turning our lives upside down, starting afresh in a new place, and figuring it out from there — together.

Peter had long been allergic to dogs and cats — especially cats. His eyes often water, and his voice constricts, when we visit friends' homes where cats also live; they always seemed drawn to him! But he grew up with dogs, so knew that there were at least some dogs with whom he could coexist. We both love dogs. I hadn't invited one into my life since Tom-dog, feeling that my work life would mean leaving a pup alone far too much.

Peter and I decided to look for a dog we could adopt and both live with. There were a few failed attempts, Peter's reactions too strong for us to keep them. These included a Great Dane puppy we named Jake, a yellow Lab named Buster, a couple of hypoallergenic breeds, and a Weimaraner with deep attachment issues, who howled heartbreakingly when we had to return him. We always arranged a trial period in which we knew we could take them back to a good home if needed.

Finally, enter Dugan.

Peter had seen a dog online at a no-kill shelter outside of Denver, so we drove over to meet him. He seemed indifferent to our presence and was overall pretty lethargic; we were disappointed. As we were preparing to leave, out of the corner of my eye, I saw a hugely energetic black-and-white springer-spaniel mix leaping excitedly against the gate of his kennel. If I had been able to attach a voice to his actions, it would have been something like, "Over here, look at me; choose me!"

We asked to meet him; the owner tried to steer us to a couple of older dogs, but we persisted. Dugan (estimated at plus or minus eighteen months) had clearly made his decision and was just waiting for us to catch up. Before leaving with him, I rubbed some of his saliva on Peter's arm, and we waited to see if there was any allergic reaction. No reaction — we had a dog…and Dugan had people and a home.

A few months later, Peter observed that Dugan seemed lonely; he did spend time at home alone when we both were at work. So we decided to get Dugan a dog of his own. We had found a breed that worked for us both, so enter Jack. The folks we bought him from had named him Lucky; he was a six-month-old purebred black-and-white springer spaniel — a little Dugan!

The young family who sold us Jack evidently thought of him as an investment, but seemed to have no idea what to do with him as a dog. They sent him off with us with his food and a bag full of stuff, including his toothbrush and Dramamine pills for riding in the car — but no toys. Once we got him home, he would only eat the same food Dugan ate. We decided it was time to let little Jack just be a dog, so threw his food and bag of stuff away.

It took a couple of weeks for Dugan to get over his indignation that Jack would sit in his chair, play with his toys, etc., but they became great friends and companions, like siblings, soon enough. The four of us became a pack; they moved with us from Colorado to New Hampshire to Southern California to Northern California, and back to Phoenix — where we — eventually and with heavy hearts — bid them both farewell — Dugan at fifteen plus, gratefully and graciously ready to peacefully take his leave, and, a year and a half later, little Jack at thirteen and a half — suddenly from an internal hemorrhage when neither he nor we were in any measure ready to see him go. It had seemed as if they were always there, at the heart of our life together, and therefore always would be, but, alas, of course, that's just not how it goes.

Nine months after losing Jack, the quiet began to outweigh the grief. We decided that we had learned how to provide a loving home for older pups — and knew that that they were often the last to get adopted. We appreciated the companionship that two dogs could offer to one another, so we set off accordingly.

Through Springer Spaniel Rescue, we identified Fenway, a shy nine-year-old, liver-and-white living in a foster home. After recovering from ACL surgery, he was ready for a new home — albeit extremely attached to his foster mom. Initially, during our visit, Fenway retreated to the safety of his crate, from which he observed his visitors keenly. As the visit proceeded and we didn't disappear, Fenway suddenly walked over to where Peter was (we were both sitting on the floor) and rolled over onto his back. Fenway had chosen his person. We formalized the arrangement with a spirited walk around the grounds and agreed that the next step would be Fenway visiting us at his new home.

We first saw Bentley on the Home Fur Good — a no-kill shelter near our home in Phoenix — website. He was a six-year-old Great Pyrenees mix with a big, fluffy tail (like Dugan's) and a black mask on his face, the rest of him pure white. He had been with the shelter for over a year and had been adopted and then returned due to occasional lunging behavior. To give him a break, staff had arranged for him to spend time with a trainer — who kindly brought him by our place for a visit.

He was, at first, aloof and disinterested as he wandered nonchalantly through the house and yard. Later, as we and the trainer sat chatting in the living room, he made the rounds to each of us, inviting pets and seeming to let us know that this would be OK with him.

We wanted to have both dogs arrive on the same day, so neither felt he had seniority over the other. There followed a visit with both of them at the house at the same time. Fenway was shy and hid behind his foster mom; Bentley took me for a brisk walk around the backyard, deposited a big dump on the lawn, and went back inside with his fluffy tail wagging.

We decided to forego crates for these guys; we had never used them with Jack and Dugan. So, their first night in their new home, Fenway settled into what had been Jack's bed, on the floor on Peter's side of the bed, and Bentley into what had been Dugan's on my side of the bed. A new pack was born. We knew at the outset that our time would be relatively brief, given their ages when we adopted them. I had a feeling that Bentley, though younger, would be the first to go, which he was, five years later in spring of 2022 — here in Southern California. Fenway followed on Christmas Eve that same year, like Bentley before him, with spirit intact but body depleted.

The four of them are our spirit pack now, waiting for us across the famous Rainbow Bridge — to reunite and show us around their new realm when our own time comes. Their remains sit on our dresser in the bedroom now, four boxes of various sizes and shapes, each with its respective occupant's collar sitting atop — ever with us.

A solitary, hardworking, hypersexed, and lonely guy before Peter entered my life, we together formed and learned family with Dugan, Jack, Fenway, and Bentley in ways and to depths that had been previously both terrifying and unimaginable to me. Even today, it seems like a dream; I can remember, and have not forgotten even a little bit, the emotionally tortured years that preceded.

Peter and I discussed making children a part of our life together and decided — for a variety of reasons — not to do so. We may or may not adopt more dogs at some point. At this writing, we're enjoying the freedom to travel and live spontaneously — while missing our spirit pups — each and every day — in all the many spaces they occupied while in the flesh…and fur.

My distance from clinical practice gave me an opportunity to reflect — and to write — about clinical issues that remained very important to me. In 2000, my chapter "Childhood Sexual Trauma in Gay Men: Social Context and the Imprinted Arousal Pattern" was published in a special volume of the *Journal of Gay and Lesbian Social Services*, titled *Gay Men and Childhood Sexual Trauma: Integrating the Shattered Self*, edited by James Cassese.

As noted, adult survivors of early-life trauma — sexual and otherwise — had become a specialty in my practice. I noticed a recurring theme in my sexual-abuse survivor clients — regardless of sexual orientation — deep confusion in their psychosexual map.

Lovemap is a term/concept coined by sexologist John Money, who also concluded from his own research that "we know as little and as much about the causes of homosexuality as we do about heterosexuality."

Gay clients wondered if they were gay because of their early abuse. Straight-male clients were confused and to some degree mortified that they also responded to same-sex fantasies and stimulation, when their abuser had been a male. Upon investigation, and comparing notes across cases, I observed that survivors — male and female — tended to respond as adults both in terms of their actual orientation...and to conditions similar to those they had experienced during their molestation. This was the imprinted arousal pattern (IAP) that I described in my 2000 chapter, a term that I coined to identify the phenomenon, and a concept that proved very helpful both to me and in treating others.

It struck me as very similar to Jung's concept of "psychic infection," a term that Jung coined in 1937 — the sufferer can transmit their psychic disease, generally via some sort of abuse, to a healthy person whose powers then — best-case scenario — subdue the demon, but not without impairing the well-being of the subduer. In the worst cases, of course, the infection can overpower the ability of the healthier psyche and be deadly.

One example: A married man in his thirties — who became, in time, a contributor to my 1995 book — had been abused for years as a boy...by a priest. He was a good and talented person with deep integrity. A reluctant client, he was referred by his wife — there for the greater good of their marriage and his desire to raise a family with the woman he loved.

Recounting the details of his abuse was painful and shameful for him — as it is with most survivors. Most difficult of all: admitting that he responded erotically as an adult to the core conditions of his abuse — an innocent younger person manipulated and seduced by an older man.

Another example: An extraordinary undergraduate — intelligent, athletic, physically stunning, articulate — also appeared reluctantly in my practice at the urging of a boyfriend who knew that my client was always "on the prowl." His early abuse began with a heterosexual adult neighbor — a "good" husband and father — wherein he felt desired and important — things he did not feel in his family. The abuse was recurring and a dark and shameful secret. His pattern thereafter was to seek out older men for whom he was a trophy or "ornament" (his word) and/or to indulge shamefully in furtive sex. A sense of true value as a person eluded him — and therefore his ability to engage in a meaningful relationship with another was impaired. His repeating patterns began to unravel when he turned thirty and noticed that younger guys were now getting the kinds of attention he had received earlier...and was no longer.

Related and basically the same dynamic manifested differently: A friend and I organized a river-rafting trip for fellow gay professional men. We were an interesting mix of physicians, psychiatrists, psychologists, and attorneys. We spent several days and nights on the American River in Northern California. As we pulled off the river the first afternoon, to set up camp and begin to prepare the evening meal, a tension that had been building between the straight guides and the gay rafters became increasingly palpable. My co-organizer and I spoke with the owner of the company, himself straight and our lead guide. We all agreed that we needed to address the issue head-on. So, the next morning — after breakfast and before we rejoined the river — we held a "fairy circle": a sacred space where we were all invited to speak — and feel — freely and openly.

We learned that some of the rafters had been bullied and brutalized as kids, by other assumed-to-be-straight boys — and that some of the guides had been molested as kids, by assumed-to-be-gay adult men. Each group projected its experience onto the other — the guides were all potential bullies, and we rafters were all potentially just lying in wait to ensnare the guides. Several men wept, never having had the experience of saying aloud what had been a dark secret. The guides were amazed at how several saw all straight men, and at how they were feared. The rafters felt so honored that our guides would share their secret pain and shame, and likewise taken aback at what was projected onto us.

The IAP here was more of an imprinted reaction pattern — instinctive, born from trauma, deeply held. Warm embraces all around — and many tears — brought our fairy circle to a close. There was no tension between guides and rafters the rest of the trip; in fact, there was warmth, great fun, and good fellowship.

In my work life, I frequently took on projects that others wouldn't, couldn't, or simply didn't. I enjoyed challenge and felt that affinity deepen progressively with each new one — starting with, as noted, leading the design and implementation process for JFKU's first doctoral program (an earlier attempt, before my tenure, had failed — this one succeeded); starting with a set of blueprints and establishing

— with Peter's essential assistance — a fully functioning and accredited multilevel-of-study Southern California campus in the for-profit sector — partly as an attractive asset in the owner's cap as he approached his company's IPO (no one else would touch the project); leading the charge to acquire Rocky Mountain College of Art and Design's first national arts accreditation and joining the owner family in locating, building out, and occupying a new campus; shepherding the New England campus of Antioch University for fifteen months as interim president, from a failed presidency to its successor — and then taking the reins of the Los Angeles campus, which I led away from a $1M deficit into a $7M surplus, while overseeing the process of design and implementation of an innovative new graduate program in urban sustainability; after serious courtship, accepting a "disruptive leadership" appointment as president of a tiny, poorly-funded, and insular alternative graduate institute and leading its transformation into a fledgling university — launching undergraduate studies, a name and branding change, and a significant expansion of the physical plant and underlying infrastructure.

Because so many of these projects were disequilibrating to the established order — rocking many boats — I learned that most folks aren't that fond of change and prefer the embrace of the status quo: a comfortable nest into which they can settle and remain — which I always, for better or worse, found a bit boring. I enjoyed making things happen, realizing visions and possibilities, creating new forms and structures. I was far too independent, outspoken, unconventional, impatient, and stubborn for many tastes. I was never content with keeping the trains running on time.

Authority figures and I were a mixed bag, no doubt due to my father's excellent role modeling. Persons in positions of authority who earned my respect and that of others working for them, I had no issue with. I respect and admire true leadership. Persons in these positions who believed that one simply obeys and questions not? Well, I tended to do less well with them.

Ironically, I myself was, in some roles, an authority figure. I attempted always to be fair, clear, and respectful, and to set appropriate boundaries. Alas, authority figures draw the projections of others relative to their own experiences with authority; the person behind the role is often not seen at all. I have always tried to keep this in mind, both in and out of the role.

While blessed to have enjoyed overwhelmingly positive and mutually respectful professional relationships throughout my career, I myself was not universally loved in the roles described above. One of my colleagues — married with two young children — complained that my "work product" put him and others to shame; another told me that he and his buddies would "chew me up and spit me out" if I followed my "history of ambition" into new leadership roles (which I did anyway); a hugely inflated graduate student told me he would "bring me to my knees" if I did not prevail upon the board of trustees to reverse a decision that he and his peers didn't like; one of my supervisors shunned me and blocked my initiatives because I was insufficiently loyal and sycophantic...and the list goes on.

Only once was I overtly confronted about my sexual orientation by an employer — in the corporate for-profit arena

— when a visiting corporate VP asked me rather brusquely, "So what's this gay thing?"

And this all was in minor-league academia — I can only imagine what it's like in the majors!

My favorite schools (ASL, RMCAD, AULA), like my favorite restaurants (Cliff House, SFBG), were the ones in which the "fit" was the best. They correlate highly with enduring friendships from workplaces.

Chapter Fifteen
Around the World, V 2.0

I collected stamps as a boy, and was enormously curious about the different countries and cultures they represented. My father's trips abroad with the navy didn't include the family; we never lived outside the USA. Aside from a couple of trips to Baja California as a college student and fledgling high school teacher, Laos was the first foreign country I decided to visit — and live and work in, in 1969. My childhood curiosity just grew from there — and became a deep, and lifelong, adult passion — enduring today.

I credit my enormous curiosity about the world and its various cultures, faiths, customs, histories, etc., as playing a major role in my survival and healing from my early life. My MO of escape, retreat, solitude, and reflection was well served by heading off into a new part of the world — figuring it out, and myself, a little more each time.

Little could I have known, when I departed Algeria in 1971, having satisfied my conscientious-objector civilian obligation as a teacher there and in Laos the prior year, how much international travel — and indeed living abroad — would shape and inform my personal and professional life for decades to come. I especially could not have divined how formative and

— in their unique way — curative these many times in foreign lands would prove to be to me.

I suspect today that so much of my becoming who I am could not have occurred otherwise, and that I could well have been at risk for the very forces that devastated other members of my family, primarily addiction. I had to escape to survive — and did so, again and again…leaving the known behind, getting outside of its reach.

I have long said that I learned more from my two years living and working in the developing world than I did in all my formal education.

As we know, I hesitated only slightly in 1977 — seven years post-Algeria — when offered a counseling position in London; leaving behind my beloved Tom-dog was my only real reservation. After London, my international travel suffered in the years that I spent in graduate school and while establishing myself professionally as a psychologist and academic. For more than a decade, I pretty much had to stay close to home to accomplish the goals I had set for myself — though never once failing to avail myself of occasional personal travel out of the USA when the opportunity presented itself during this time.

In 2001, I was invited by a Taiwanese couple, whom I knew professionally in Southern California, to accompany them to China as a consultant; they had a vision of establishing an American-curriculum secondary school there and wanted my assistance. As far as I know, their vision was never realized, BUT the contacts I made in China while with them proved very useful later.

As provost of Rocky Mountain College of Art and Design (RMCAD) in Colorado, I learned that the school was interested in establishing exchange programs in Asia. I led two delegations from RMCAD to the same Central China/Henan Province universities I had visited on my first trip. On the second visit, we mounted Henan University's first-ever exhibition of Western Art, which had been juried by RMCAD faculty, and included work from students and faculty — including one of my photographs.

Soon after, as academic dean of the New England campus of Antioch University, I led a delegation back to China with similar intent, in 2005, during which we established an exchange program with privately owned Sias International University, coincidentally also in Henan Province — and offered them an initial full scholarship to get the program established.

I was appointed president of Antioch University Los Angeles (AULA) in 2007. Iconic portraitist Don Bachardy honored us by allowing an extensive exhibition of his recent work to be a key part of the inaugural festivities. Don presided with his characteristic elegance and grace at the standing-room-only opening.

As AULA president, I became one of the founding members of a new organization, LGBTQ Presidents in Higher Education — currently broadened to become LGBTQ Leaders In Higher Education. Our numbers as out college presidents nationally were miniscule at the time. There were perhaps six or eight of us in the beginning.

Our first meeting was hosted in Chicago by then Roosevelt University President Chuck Middleton. I hosted the second meeting at AULA, during which we collectively — with our partners — filmed a powerful *It Gets Better* video as a message to young members of the LGBTQ community struggling with their sexual identities.

This was, for me, a pivotal moment of individuation and integration: throwing off the shame in which my early life had entangled my sexuality, and joining my private life with my public life.

In 2009, during my tenure as AULA president, I received an invitation for a North American University Presidents retreat from IAUP — to be held in Chicago. I had never heard of IAUP at the time, but was interested in seeing what they might have to offer by way of potential exchange programs for AULA…and welcomed the chance to visit with AULA alumni who lived in the Chicago area.

The retreat's host was the aforementioned Dr. J. Michael Adams, then president of Fairleigh Dickinson University (FDU) in New Jersey, and president-elect of IAUP for the 2011–2014 term of office. We hit it off immediately; he encouraged me to become involved with the organization…and his impending presidency. He offered me appointment, then and there, to the IAUP Executive Committee during his term. I was, of course, flattered, and said I'd seek clearance from my board and supervisor at Antioch to attend the next international meeting, set for Tokyo the next year.

So 2010 found me on Tokyo Bay, chatting with Fidel Ramos, former president of the Philippines, on board a ship chartered for our gala dinner to conclude the IAUP regional meeting hosted by Japanese member universities. It also found me in New York, at the United Nations, for the launch of the UN Academic Impact, a joint UN-IAUP initiative. Presiding at the launch were Michael and then UN Secretary-General Ban Ki-moon. Afterwards, sitting in the UN cafeteria with Michael and two of his FDU colleagues, Michael stunned me by asking me to join his IAUP administration as his number two, secretary-general — essentially the COO who was responsible for traveling to various locations around the world to do the advance work needed with local host universities where regional meetings would later be held.

After another round of consultation at home — both with Peter and with the university — I found myself in Casablanca in 2011, being introduced to the IAUP Executive Committee as the incoming secretary-general, set to take office later that year with Michael. Peter and I realized and accepted that this new commitment to IAUP would take me away from home at least a couple of times a year. My responsibilities with IAUP were embraced by the board of my new university as both an opportunity for the school and a badge of honor.

By the time IAUP gathered in New York in 2011, for its triennial meeting and the change of administrations, I had left Antioch University. Hundreds of university presidents from around the world gathered to confer, learn, have fun together, make connections, and form alliances. Michael presided with grace and authority and was clearly very highly regarded. He had, by then, been with IAUP for a decade and knew the organization and its members well.

At the time of the Triennial Conference, I had no idea that Michael was suffering from jaw cancer...and certainly not that he would be dead in a year's time...barely into his term of office and while still the sitting president of both IAUP and FDU.

Michael had worked mightily to prepare IAUP for his presidency, and he had a grand and well-conceived vision — designed to endure for years — for the organization. He effectuated a change of the governance structure at the

New York Triennial, which included establishing a fiduciary board of directors. He had been able to attend the first gathering — in Doha, in 2010 — of the World Innovation Summit for Education (WISE), for which IAUP, under his leadership, had been a partner to the Qatar Foundation. I was also a member of the inaugural IAUP delegation.

By the second WISE gathering in 2011, Michael was too ill to travel. I unofficially took on many of his responsibilities in addition to my own. He was not able to attend the first regional meetings of his term — in Vienna and Bogota. Instead, I consulted closely with him while he was convalescing at home — and presided in his place — giving updates on his health to our assembled colleagues. We were all then hoping for a full recovery, despite that seeming less and less likely as time went on.

I traveled to see Michael at his home in New Jersey — he was gaunt and needed to rest for periods during our visit — but we made some key decisions together, and he clearly enjoyed my coming to see him. I did not see him again. Instead, we began our next regional meeting, in Tbilisi, with a moment of silence for Michael, after which members present shared memories and reactions to his passing.

The board asked me to formally assume the role of president for the remainder of Michael's term, which I agreed to do — knowing well that this would mean a great deal of additional travel and time away from work and home. I felt that I owed it to Michael to do what I could to carry out his vision and to cement his legacy.

After Michael's memorial at FDU, at which Ban Ki-moon was the first speaker and I the second, I accepted Ban Ki-moon's invitation for a private meeting at the UN — in order to honor and seek to perpetuate the deep relationship that Michael had established with the UN and the secretary-general's office. I added meetings, board and committee memberships, and speaking engagements at the UN and elsewhere to my schedule, while continuing with my advance work for the term's remaining regional meetings — in Oxford, Guadalajara, San Juan, and Montego Bay.

I continued with my day job in California — routinely making my trips out of state and abroad as brief as possible — and was promptly at my desk the morning after my return, jet lag be damned.

In 2014, Yokohama was the site of the Triennial Conference, and the three-year presidency transferred to my Japanese colleague, Dr. Toyoshi Sato — preceded by a meeting in London of the new board, with our attorney and financial advisors, to school us all on the governance structure and our collective duties and responsibilities.

Per the newly established governance structure, the immediate past president became the chair of the board of directors for the succeeding three-year term as the new president took office — a role that Michael had looked forward to for himself. That same year, I resigned my last university presidency and entered into a private consulting practice with a colleague.

Bill Clinton was still president when I first encountered him in person — at a rally for Al Gore, in LA, in 2000. The small crowd roared when his familiar shock of white hair appeared as he ascended the rear stairs to the stage. I was struck immediately at his alert, curious gaze — taking it all in — before he spoke off the cuff. I next encountered him at two meetings of the Clinton Global Initiative University, during which he addressed college presidents in attendance at a private luncheon. Attendees included president colleagues of mine from IAUP and from Antioch University. He made the rounds of the room, shaking each of our hands.

After the second meeting's luncheon, as staff were gently nudging him toward the door and on to his next engagement, he lingered to receive individual attendees who had queued up to have a private word with him. I decided to thank him personally for his then-recent public support of gay marriage. Clinton ignored the staff member at his elbow and we engaged in a prolonged handshake for a brief conversation, during which he read my name tag and gave me his undivided attention — the famous you-are-the-only-person-in-the-room experience he was noted for.

Our next meetings were in Arizona, both at fundraisers for his wife's ill-fated 2016 campaign for president. During the first, I met and established a good connection with Connie, who oversaw advance work for this visit, and traveled with the then former president in his motorcade — and again shook hands and exchanged a few words with Mr. Clinton. For the second event, Connie asked if I would join her advance team — and if Peter would be willing to drive the press vehicle in the motorcade. We both agreed.

I was a part of the small welcoming party when Mr. Clinton arrived at the event; he clearly by then remembered me, came over, and said it was nice to see me again, expressed apologies for running late, and was eager to speak with those assembled to meet him. Peter and I were later invited to join the (quick-moving) line to have a photograph taken with the former president.

Bill Clinton's relevance to this tale? I see him as a brilliant and imperfect trauma survivor who carried not-fully-resolved parts of his early life — and his secret life — into his personal and professional lives. I didn't always agree with him politically, but thought that he — perhaps unwittingly — provided important life lessons to others of us who were grappling with integrating our early lives — public, private, and secret — with our contemporary lives.

Peter's father died in late 2011, in Florida; soon afterwards, his mother moved to Phoenix to be closer to her daughters, both of whom had settled in the area. In 2014, Peter and I moved back to Phoenix as well, buying a house in our old neighborhood. For the first time since they all left home, Peter's mother, Grace, now a new widow, had all three kids nearby. We stayed for the next six-plus years — the summers getting hotter for longer periods of time as the planet warmed. I was not in love with the Southwest this time around. Scorpions became a scourge — we both got stung more than once.

Still with IAUP — and simply flying out of a different airport — I was no longer preparing for regional meetings, but rather attending them...and chairing the board meeting held at each one. South Africa, Australia, Prague, and Madrid hosted the Japanese presidency's regional meetings. I was also called to represent the organization — often as panelist, presenter, and/or keynote speaker — at meetings and conferences in China, Taiwan, Saudi Arabia (I obtained consultation on the wisdom of traveling here as a gay man before this trip),

Brazil, and Denmark during this time. I also continued with some of my UN duties.

Finally, in 2017, the Triennial Conference having taken place in Vienna, the presidency passed to a charismatic young man from Tbilisi, Dr. Kakha Shengelia — for whom Michael had been an important mentor. I rotated off the board and handed off my UN roles to Kakha.

The confident independence that became central to my identity, I attribute to my early life and the quickly internalized realization that I was on my own and had to figure out the road ahead. There was no map; it was sink or swim — with a little treading water here and there. My years as a young educator in Laos, Algeria, and London had served me well in the most unanticipated context of IAUP.

Living and working in multiple countries and cultures, together with my study of Jung and his concept of the collective unconscious, underpin my cosmology / concept of spirituality today: we are one spirit, individual cells of the same ineffable and divine being — our religions all noble, but ultimately inadequate, attempts to master the mystery. In this sense, I'm a Taoist — the mystery is greater than our capacity to understand it.

I was quite happy to surrender my remaining international roles after the Vienna meeting, after which Peter, who had accompanied me to this and the Australia meetings, and I traveled by train to Venice for some days of pure R and R.

By the time my peripatetic, professional international travel came to its conclusion, I had visited over fifty-five countries and logged over one million air miles — earning Peter and me Star Alliance Gold status for life.

The expected news that Sharon had died in hospice, in San Diego, found us in our last days in Venice. We had said our goodbyes before this last IAUP trip, and I was quite certain that I would not see her again. Six months prior to her death, I had turned seventy; she would have turned sixty-seven two months after.

I really didn't want to write this next section. It threatened to bring it all back while still tender…and drive home the immutability of her demise. I procrastinated more than is my usual wont and discovered multiple urgent tasks that suddenly required my immediate attention, etc. But ultimately… here we are…

Sharon's final chapter was long and painful — and absent her normal grace, humor, and dignity. She had struggled all her adult life with the family curse, addiction — alcohol mostly, but she hit the cocaine pretty hard when they were dealing, and became fairly indiscriminate at the end. The curse's incredibly merciless and tenacious tendrils ensnared and ultimately destroyed her, her struggles against notwithstanding.

She managed to pretty much keep it all in check, when my niece was growing up, and was a devoted and responsible mother. She was courageous in the face of her initial breast-cancer diagnosis in the very early 2000s, driving herself to and from excruciating chemo sessions.

She finally divorced her husband — who was privately a very angry man, as our father had been, and had become an out-of-control speed addict — a total 180 from his previously evangelical abstention from all intoxicating substances. She kept the house, and he got much of the cash. He terrorized his former wife and daughter during some of his worst episodes. He showed up — sheepishly and unexpectedly — at his daughter's high school graduation in 2000, sitting alone — apart from the rest of us. He died a horrible death in 2010 — walking at night, while reportedly very high, on the I-5 freeway near his late parents' home in Old Town San Diego; he was sixty years old. I don't believe that Sharon ever recovered from his death.

She and Leia drove over for Thanksgiving in 2014, the year we returned to Phoenix; she visited one other time, flying over on her own. She always checked a bag rather than just do carry-on, even for a short visit — that way she could carry and conceal a bottle in her luggage. Our aunt Jeanne was visiting during Sharon's second trip over, and Sharon took us all to lunch. She loved Peter — and us as a couple.

Her deterioration began in earnest shortly thereafter. She began showing up intoxicated to work; they eventually very generously and graciously ushered her into early retirement, her benefits intact. Unfortunately, with all that free time, and shamed by her forced retirement, her drinking only intensified.

One of the gifts of our being back in Phoenix, and my time having become my own, was that I could visit Sharon frequently in San Diego. On one visit, she wasn't responding to texts or calls, so I simply showed up at her place. Startled, she tried at first to hide the brown paper bag holding her vodka bottle, but then just relaxed into her stupor. We agreed to meet later; she was passed out on the couch when I returned.

I was sometimes harsh with her during this time — in a tough-love vein — to little avail. She methodically pushed people out of her life, the better to be alone with her bottle. There was never any doubt that this would not fly with me.

By 2015, her breast cancer had returned, and she had been diagnosed with non-Hodgkin's lymphoma and liver cancer. I accompanied her to several hospital visits during this time. She had become noncompliant with her medication. On one visit, when the physician attempted to counsel her back toward treatment, she simply got up and walked out. I found her later crumpled up in the back seat of her car.

She had given up. She drank nonstop, often passing out somewhere in her neighborhood. She was in and out of rehab programs, where she'd sober up…until the moment she was out again. Her insurance limited the duration of her rehab stays.

We maintained our Sunday-morning phone calls, a ritual for decades. They became brief and desultory. I flew over for her sixty-fifth birthday, September 15, 2015; we planned to go out to dinner. Instead, I greeted the paramedics at her place; Leia had summoned them after Sharon did a face-plant on the rear patio, her solo birthday celebration having started a bit early. It was not her first ambulance ride during this dark home stretch.

I drove out to collect her a few hours later at the hospital. On the drive home, she was vile and hateful toward Leia… and asked me if we could still go out to dinner. Deeply saddened, I left her at home and took myself to dinner. The next morning, she had little recall of — and no shame for — the prior day's events.

Her home became increasingly squalid and her day-to-day more and more grotesque. Her poor daughter became her primary caregiver, a terrible burden and responsibility. Eventually, there followed a series of group homes; she was no longer capable of managing her own life. She was at least sober during our visits, and conversation was possible, albeit limited; she became childlike — clearly significantly cognitively diminished.

On one visit, Peter and I collected her and took her with us to see Leia's graduation play at San Diego State University. Leia was a theater major — backstage, props and the like. I pushed Sharon in a wheelchair to and from the theater; she had difficulty following the play and tried to manipulate me afterwards into taking her back to her home — where I'm guessing she believed that one of her stashed bottles still awaited her. We left her back at the group home.

Sharon's last stop was a shared hospice room — in a nondescript house, in a nondescript San Diego neighborhood a few miles from her home. It was a brief stay. I was only there to visit a couple of times before Peter and I took off for Vienna and Venice.

She always lit up and was delighted to see me during our final visits. On our last one, as I held her hand, she drifted in and out of consciousness, occasionally registering my presence. Just as I was preparing to leave, we were blessed with a brief window of clarity and connection. We both told the other that we loved them; it was my last time looking into those dark-blue eyes that had grounded me my entire life. I kissed her lightly on the forehead and took my leave — turning to look at her one more time as I walked out the door; she was again unconscious.

Days later — July 10, 2017 — she was gone.

As soon as Peter and I returned to the States, I drove over to be with Leia; Sharon had died eight days before Leia's thirty-fourth birthday, so we marked both events in the same visit. Leia was able to acknowledge both her relief and her grief.

If someone were to have experienced Sharon only toward the end of her life, they would have no idea how much her final years fundamentally and utterly disfigured this tough and tender, always feisty, courageous, playful/mischief-prone, delicate, and gently powerful soul. I choose to remember her as I knew her over the totality of her life, and not as the aberration that was her exit. We were great friends — we liked, loved, and enjoyed one another — immensely.

A few months after Sharon died, I took a solo "Sharon Memorial Drive" over to the California Central Coast — to visit places where she had been happy. In Morro Bay, I stood above the back bay, where she and Eugene had lived on a Chinese junk together, before Leia was born. I drove over to walk around Morro Rock, fenced off now, where we used to hike around to the ocean side and smoke weed.

On one of our visits to Morro Rock, Tom-dog was amongst us; when we rounded the final curve to the ocean side, a seal was sunning on the rocks. Tom had a very expressive face. He shot me a very startled look, then a puzzled one, then an absolutely amazed one as the seal slid back into the water.

I parked across from the gated entrance to their San Simeon property and watched the current owner arrive, unlock the gate, and drive up the familiar road leading to what had once been their home — where infant Leia spent her first years in a wooden crib I had given them and later named one of the resident ducks Uncle Neal.

I drove by our parents' home, where Sharon's water broke and Roy died; I found a contractor and his crew there, remodeling it for sale — after the people we sold it to nearly thirty years prior had themselves died. He graciously allowed me to walk through it with him and see the various changes he was making. It was soothing to revisit these earlier parts of Sharon's life and realize that I had not imagined all that preceded her sad final years.

In my view, we two had best managed to craft a full-ish adult life for ourselves out of the ruins of our childhood. She lived almost twenty years longer than Ken, and more than a dozen more than our mother.

Writing about her dying is like saying goodbye all over again. She was different from the others; we had planned to have fun together as old people. I miss her terribly. She was the last with whom I could share stories, validate memories, commiserate over and celebrate surviving our nuclear family. She deserved better than what life delivered to her.

Recently, during this writing, word reached me that a close cousin's son had died at age fifty-three, after a lifetime's struggle with addictions, leaving four wonderful young-adult children behind, the birth of his first grandchild imminent.

Sharon was not the end of the line to suffer the multigenerational family curse.

Chapter Sixteen
Chapters Ending and Beginning

Looking back, I can see now that 2017 was quite a significant year of passage, chapters ending and new ones beginning.

Sharon had died; I rotated off the board of IAUP and ended my nine-year, peripatetic involvement with them, which also marked the end of my formal work life. I rarely put on a tie after this time. Dugan and Jack both left us; I had turned seventy.

In terms of new beginnings: life after seventy; the reality of retirement; Bentley and Fenway entered our life together; a kind of tyrannical freedom took hold, which at first felt like an all-enveloping fog. Who was I, and what was I to do now?

It was a few years yet before COVID hit; I knew that I wanted to leave Arizona and return to California, but also knew that the time was not yet right to do so.

There was a new period of flailing, vastly different from the one that defined my early life. Striving had always been at the core of my being: striving to escape my family and my shame; striving to excel and thereby prove myself; striving as a kind of drug that I could always count on to motivate and excite me and point me in new directions — away from the trauma of my early life and all the ways I felt diminished, afflicted, and, indeed, stunted by it.

So I found myself at seventy with my striving "engine" still running, per usual, but having no clear direction for its energies. I tried volunteering at various organizations: a political campaign, a no-kill animal shelter, a local church that offered sanctuary to newly arrived immigrants who were not yet legal, an organization for gay youth, another for homeless youth. Nothing really took hold.

My consulting work came to feel…well…too much like work — and I gradually realized that I was tired of work, didn't have to work anymore, and could simply chill — whatever that meant.

In time, I realized too that I was deeply tired, a lifetime of tired, worn out spiritually and emotionally from my constant vigilance and strategies to escape, again and again…tired.

Part V

View from
the Terrace

Chapter Seventeen
Context Revisited – From Then to Now

My parents were born into the aftermath of WWI; their parents then had to navigate the Great Depression. Both were forces that shaped my parents' young lives — and to which they would have been oblivious at the time. All working class, none of my grandparents finished more than a high school education — and I'm not sure how many of them even got that far. At the time of their deaths, they owned their own modest properties — something that their parents had not achieved.

I don't recall any Great Depression stories from my mother's side of the family, but heard about my father and his brothers being publicly shamed by having to scavenge for coal along the railroad tracks to keep the family warm, and about there often not being enough to eat.

When I visited my paternal grandparents, from LA as a high school student, I had become accustomed to walking around barefoot and had developed thick calluses on the bottom of my feet. My grandmother was aghast, my shoelessness implying the very poverty they had worked so hard to overcome. She insisted that I wear my shoes.

My siblings and I were born into the aftermath of WWII; our family was buoyed into the middle class by the nation's postwar prosperity. Though he did not experience combat first-hand, my father served in both WWII and the Korean War. The navy sent him to specialized training, including a two-year course at UCLA, but neither parent earned a college degree — though both did complete high school. Between the two world wars, FDR enacted the New Deal. As we've seen above, my parents bought their first house, a 3/2 with two-car garage, in San Pedro, for $15,000 — in 1956. Television sets became ubiquitous in American homes; as I mentioned earlier, we had several. They owned their homes for the rest of their lives.

We three were as oblivious to the macro forces that shaped our lives as our parents had been to their own as children.

I am the sole person from my family to earn a college degree — let alone three degrees. Sharon did complete her AA, and Ken received specialized training in the navy's nuclear program. My high-school senior year saw the assassination of John Kennedy and the arrival of the Beatles in the USA a few months after.

My senior year at SMC saw the assassinations of Martin Luther King Jr. and Robert Kennedy. The nation was in turmoil over the Vietnam War; many college campuses were in open revolt. My response to the Vietnam War — as we've seen — was to declare myself a conscientious objector to all war, embracing a lifelong pacifism that has put me at odds with many in my family and amongst my contemporaries. As I mentioned earlier, this was one of two times that my father disowned me (the other, later, was when Norma — who is African American — and I announced plans to marry), to which I was utterly indifferent. My father and older brother retired from the navy as junior officers, each after twenty-plus years of service, having worked their way up the ranks.

Today, internationally, we are awash in nuclear weapons — some held and controlled in nations ruled by despots. There are enough, in aggregate, to destroy all life on the planet — many times over. The major powers support proxies in wars that they dare not engage directly, lest those weapons be unleashed.

Ukraine and Gaza are the sites of the current major international conflicts; there have been, and surely will be, others tomorrow. Once again, many college campuses are in open revolt at this writing, pitting pro-Israeli against pro-Palestinian.

TikTok influencers make enormous incomes, and many young people have OnlyFans accounts where they charge admission for witnessing their sexual activity online.

People disagree how many genders there are. I meet for coffee once a month with two neighbors, one born in 1937 and the other in 1950. The elder one tells us about his transexual grandson, born biologically female, since transitioned, and having adopted a male name and pronouns. The younger gentleman tells us about his own, nonbinary grandson who happens also to be on the autism spectrum and uses *we / they* as their pronouns. They use a female name at school and a male name at home. Both men laugh at themselves as they struggle with identities, realities, and pronouns to which they are not accustomed.

The political center in most Western countries has disappeared, their politics sharply divided. An ever-intensifying epidemic of gun violence has been a fact of life for over a quarter century in the USA. Western Europe seems to be steadily drifting rightward.

Forces on the right seek to reverse FDR's New Deal and many of the more progressive social movements that it birthed, while the left seeks to perpetuate what it sees as the societal gains of the last several decades. The right seems to stand for a consolidation of wealth and power, while the left seeks to distribute both more broadly. An underlying demographic tension is the shrinking Caucasian population against the growing non-European descendant population, with many of those with European roots feeling, ironically, that our still-young nation is "theirs" — and that all others are unwelcome interlopers.

People born into today's world will inhabit a dangerously warming planet, in which the gaps between rich and poor have never been greater. Many are being born to parents who struggle to find affordable housing, even in the world's advanced economies. They, like their parents, will be "digital natives" — will have never known a pre-Internet reality. As such, they will encounter daily an onslaught of stimulation, imagery, predation, and need for discernment that will often be well beyond their maturational level. They also — like their parents, my own parents, and me — will be oblivious to the macro forces shaping the lives they are about to begin.

There is an unprecedented awareness of, and vigilance against, exploitation of women and children — sexual and otherwise. Powerful individuals and institutions have been held accountable for their actions in this regard; others continue to evade accountability.

Trauma — collective, familial, individual — remains ubiquitous with a certain stubborn tenacity; it is a fact and aspect of life for many across generations, cultures, and societies.

Mine is of course but one story, but I learned long ago that I am not alone.

The View from the Terrace

Palm Springs became a frequent stopping-off point when I'd drive from Phoenix to San Diego to visit Sharon in her later years and, afterwards, to visit Leia. I'd invariably spend an enjoyable evening with Ray and Jerry — always full of stories and reminiscences, plentiful wine, and lots of laughter. Peter has gotten to know these rascals as well; Jerry took to calling Peter "the ingenue" (my old honorific) and my "Edwardian gentleman." As we later learned, these were their final years as well.

I'd heard for some time about the "back way" through the mountains from Palm Springs to San Diego, but it was only during this period that I actually drove it for the first time — and then several other. It's a magnificent drive, one we enjoy today. Coming west, the route takes you through Anza, then drops you down into the Temecula Valley before you reach the Interstate 15 South into San Diego.

I grew up in Southern California, Sharon lived in San Diego for years, and Peter and I lived in LA and Orange County during my working life. We had never heard of — and knew nothing about — the Temecula Valley. I was struck at the area's physical beauty and the fact that it possessed most of the retail amenities we were accustomed to: COSTCO, Sprouts, Trader Joe's, etc. I also learned, upon further investigation, that real estate was — for a desirable area in Southern California — relatively affordable.

I mentioned these observations to Peter and then pretty much filed them away, as moving out of Phoenix was not in the cards as long as his family were all in residence there. But then — surprise, surprise — in 2020, his two sisters and their husbands sold their Arizona properties and moved to the Northwoods of Wisconsin, where one of the husbands had property and a family history.

The Phoenix real estate market had gotten quite hot (pun intended) — despite the increasingly unbearable summer heat and the dwindling water supply for the region. So, long story short, we sold too and moved to the Temecula Valley, Fenway and Bentley in tow, closing on our new home here in early November 2020, just after the elections. Peter's mother followed suit soon thereafter, clear that she wanted neither to stay on her own in Phoenix, nor endure Wisconsin winters. Today, she and we live ten minutes apart, and the Wisconsinites appear for visits shortly after the first snow at home.

The region boasts fifty-plus wineries — something we had only the slightest inkling of when we decided to move here. As it happens, we like wine — my family's relationship to alcohol notwithstanding. We are still amazed that this elegant Tuscanesque countryside is only minutes from our home. We visit our favorite wineries regularly and delight in taking visitors for tastings.

And as our realtor pointed out when we were searching here, we're an hour from everywhere — as long as everywhere means Palm Springs, San Diego, or spots along the Pacific Coast. It's a bit longer to LA, and the traffic can be horrific. We often get a most welcome ocean breeze and/or morning marine layer — sometimes as thick as a London fog. There can be a light and infrequent freeze in the winter months, and summer days occasionally top 100 degrees — which neighbors consider hot, but we, having not forgotten our Arizona summers, do not. Summer evenings cool down considerably here — something they do not do in Phoenix. One often sees hot-air balloons on the near horizon in the early morning, usually in the eastern sky. Recently, two flew low directly over our house; we could wave to those on board, and them to us.

While the cities of Murrieta and Temecula proper each come in at more or less 100,000 souls, the larger metro area is in the neighborhood of one million — and growing rapidly. Commuter traffic is heavy in the mornings, south toward San Diego on Interstate 15, and inversely the same headed north later in the day. Fortunately, we both have done our time with that thankless ritual.

The San Pedro house I grew up in is roughly ninety miles to the northwest; Sharon's last residence, and Leia's current one, is about sixty miles south.

While I no longer practice psychotherapy, I have maintained my California psychologist license, in inactive status, since I closed my practice in Berkeley in 1997. I retain a small consulting practice, in which I focus on "life transitions" — organizational, familial, and individual. I earned my credentials here from the university of real life — my favorite and best teacher. From time to time, a former student or client will get in touch for consultation.

I last worked at a "job" in 2014. I'm one of those for whom retirement was a gradual — and somewhat difficult

— adjustment; but I've come to absolutely love my time being entirely my own, to do with as I please.

A neighbor recently made a comment about retirement that resonated: "Your identity is no longer what you do or did; it's now who you are as a person."

I think we may have finally settled down, ironically full circle, back to the Southern California of my youth. I wish wistfully that the old Sharon still lived an hour down the road; we'd have been frequent visitors.

Here in my study — where I write most mornings — are, unwittingly arrayed in the corner where my desk also sits, artwork by deceased loved ones — Sharon, Nick, Michael, Dan (an excellent painter and former boyfriend in San Francisco, of whom I was very fond and who died from AIDS) — and, nearby, family photographs — Dugan, Jack, Bentley, and Fenway; our family of five; plus my mother's parents, who would have been visiting from Massachusetts, with me holding Cookie, in front of the San Pedro house; Ken's, Sharon's, and my high school graduation photos, all in one frame; lots of Sharon and Leia over the years; etc.

The photograph of the five of us standing more or less in a row in front of the San Pedro house — early 1960s — encapsulates so much of this tale; it strikes me as remarkable that it even exists today. Bespectacled Ken — then long and lean at seventeen, plus or minus, towering above the rest of us at six foot three — stands slightly off to himself on the right, his hands behind his back. I'm the other brother-bookend, fifteenish, standing slightly off to the left (as far as I can be from my father and still be in the photo), holding Cookie, whose face is obscured in shadow. Between us, right to left, are my grandmother Macklin, arms by her side, essentially shoulder to shoulder with her daughter; Roy standing behind them, face and torso appearing between. Ellen is largely obscured as well, wearing aviator sunglasses, her hair not styled but combed back as she often wore it in those days. Sharon, twelve or so, diminutive at not even her full adult height of five feet, stands directly in front of our mother, looking shyly down, in a dark dress with pink polka dots, her blonde hair carefully arranged. Uncharacteristically, in what looks forced and awkward, even here, Ellen's right-hand rests on Sharon's right shoulder. Otherwise, no one is touching anyone. Both Sharon and Ellen look somewhat uncomfortable. Between Ellen and me, continuing to the left, stands my grandfather Macklin, Ellen's father, also with his hands behind his back. We all look very serious; only my grandmother sports even the slightest smile.

I have no idea who took the photo. It belies so many secrets — I'm guessing that Roy alone knew all or most of them — and so many tensions that lived under the surface in our day-to-day. It's the only family portrait that I possess today. I don't think that there were ever many others.

There's a photo of Ken, Sharon, Roy, and me at Ken's navy retirement ceremony in San Diego, in October 1990 — a few weeks before Roy died. This too is fascinating. Sharon, trim and smartly dressed in a navy-blue suit and pink blouse, stands to the right of the group. She's holding some sort of plaque that Ken was just awarded. I'm to her right in a V-neck white sweater, khaki pants, and a light-blue shirt. My right hand is in my pants pocket, my left holding a folder from the ceremony. Sharon and I are smiling slightly. The two lieutenant commanders, both a bit portly here, are to my right, Roy wearing an untucked red shirt and brown trousers, hands at his side. Ken's at the end, in uniform, hands at his side as well — looking as if he's trying to smile. He's leaving the navy after twenty-six years of service and has no plan for the future — which turns out to be tragically brief.

A year and half later, only Sharon and I were left.

Don Bachardy's searingly insightful portrait of Peter graces one wall, the old green-leather couch that lived in my Berkeley office for years — and upon which all four dogs have napped — lies beneath. One of my photographs — of a naked young man underwater — accompanies other artwork on the opposite wall. Gifts from my SMC classmates and colleagues in Denver, LA, and Phoenix cohabit with mementos from countries visited over the decades. The bookcases house the professional and personal works most dear to me: from politics, education, psychology, genealogy, and photography, to works of poetry, art, fiction, and biography — and include my own publications to date.

A porcelain Hotei, Japanese god of happiness, ironically acquired by my father when he visited Japan while in the navy, sits a couple of shelves above the family photo in San Pedro. He stood as mute witness to my entire childhood; we get to hang out together today, survivors both.

There's a black-and-white photo taken in Laos; I'm standing between two of my robed Buddhist-monk friends, Maha Khamphan on my right and Maha Swath on my left. The traditional Berber vase that Rabah gave me when we visited his mother's house in Algeria, my presidential medal from

AULA, and a couple of small and minor Keith Harings also adorn the walls and shelves.

Just outside my study window, we planted a camellia bush — my mother's favorite; she had them planted in the front entry to the San Pedro house.

My past surrounds and intertwines my present, but is a visitor now — and I am no longer its captive.

As Peter and I always have, we enjoy cordial relations with our neighbors; we've adopted the custom of exchanging holiday treats with several; we watch over one another's homes when one is away, lend a hand when needed, etc. We inherited a rose garden in our side yard, from three owners ago; it had been a bit neglected, but I'm trying to both augment it and bring it back to full health. It has a way to go to equal Vera Valentine's prize garden in London, but I'm giving it my best shot.

We've had the large front lawn we inherited removed, and have relandscaped the yard in more sustainable fashion with a large array of flowering plants. My cousin Paul declared, when he first saw the results, "It looks like a park." We both putter, plant, and prune as needed. We delight in visits from hummingbirds, bees, and Monarch butterflies. Much of the year, we're able to take meals outside.

We are quite blessed to be able to live comfortably, while not extravagantly, and to travel, entertain, and recreate pretty much as we please. Peter has fallen in love with pickleball — which he describes as "amazingly fun" — and plays most mornings, while able — at the same time — to accommodate his working-from-home work schedule. On our daily mile-or-so walk to the neighborhood dog park and back, we invariably greet/visit with neighbors along the way and, more importantly, get our dog fix when we get to see our many canine friends at the park.

Humbled by sufficient arthritis — and years of skin cancer treatments for the sun worship of my Southern California youth — to remind me that I am subject to the same vagaries of aging as the next person — it is not lost on me, in the least, that in my case I get to enjoy and embrace this experience, where so many others have not been so blessed.

May Sarton's *At Seventy: A Journal* was published in 1987; I was forty and marveled that someone so old could still write a book. Jan Morris published her *In My Mind's Eye: A Thought Diary* in 2018, when she was ninety-two, and I was seventy-one. I was inspired by, and loved reading, this memoir and sent her a note in her beloved Wales telling her so — and promising that if I was fortunate enough to live into my nineties and still have my wits about me, I would still be writing — in her honor. She was kind enough to send me back a note on the book's publication card that said simply, "Neal King, Thank You," on one side and, "Love and thanks from Wales and Jan M. on a rainy Welsh evening!" on the other.

As mentioned above, C. G. Jung's *The Red Book* sits — still shrink-wrapped — atop a bookcase here in my study. It's being saved, admittedly somewhat presumptuously, for me to unwrap and savor in my eighties.

I was able to enjoy multiple very-rich conversations with faculty colleagues about our respective "cosmologies" — where and how we fit in the great mystery, and how we think and feel about this question. I'm one of those who considers himself deeply spiritual, but not in the least religious.

Peter has long loved tennis, and was in fact a professional tennis umpire when we met. I was at best a mediocre player in high school, but have since come to love and be fascinated by the game and the top echelon of professional players — all remarkable athletes. We had great tickets to see Rafa Nadal play brilliantly — as he came back from injury — in the French Open in 2013 and got to stand at Centre Court in Wimbledon — albeit with no play in progress — in 1999. My hope is that we will have traveled back to Australia in 2027 to celebrate thirty years together, and my eightieth, by attending the Australian Open that year in Sydney.

I'm hoping to surpass my paternal grandmother's almost-ninety-five years of life, and to keep Peter company as long as I am able. I rather like the idea of being the family's first centenarian — hopefully still vital in body, mind, and spirit.

Sometime during my twenties, in an airport I don't remember where, I encountered a nattily dressed elderly man — tweed jacket and bow tie — sitting in a wheelchair, waiting to board his flight to Paris for his ninety-fifth birthday. He inspired me then and inspires me now.

Peter and I are both homebodies and introverts. I knew Nick for many years before he got that I actually am shy by nature. Likewise, it wasn't until I retired and could drop the extrovert-as-needed mask that had served me so well over the years that even Peter got that I, too, am an introvert. I was delighted in his surprise that I am actually more of an introvert by nature than he is. Norma once commented that she found me and the life I lived at the time "monkish."

In my professional life — much of which Peter witnessed and/or participated in directly — you could hand me a microphone in front of a thousand people, and I was right at home — as long as I had a role to play and imagined that I had something worth saying. But then — as now — drop me into a social situation and ask me to make small talk, and I'm an abject failure.

My family-hero role with its paradoxical need to escape — and provide cover for — my family, plus the reinforcement I got across settings as a sociable public speaker in various leadership roles, all congealed to create the persona of the comfortable extrovert — whose masking of what lie beneath was rarely even suspected.

Jung posited that our psyche possesses both the animus, or unconscious masculine side of a woman, and the anima, or unconscious feminine side of a man. Only in the second half of life do the unconscious side of each emerge into consciousness, moving us essentially toward balance and wholeness. A man finds himself embracing his anima, and a woman her animus. I think about this concept as I now putter around the house, tend the roses — with an ever-vigilant effort to enforce my aphids-not-allowed policy — and overall focus much more on domesticity than the external world.

At the same time, I'm aware that by today's definitions of gender(s) — inherently fluid and including the nonbinary — this concept may seem and feel a bit outdated.

I still, in all honestly, abhor cleaning the house.

Chapter Eighteen
Where Did Everyone Go?

Amongst a still somewhat-tangled web of often conflicting emotion, I continue to possess today an underlying survivor's guilt in my comfortable Southern California life with Peter... while so many departed so much earlier, many of their lives truncated by demons they could not exorcise. Who am I to get to still be here?

My survivor's guilt intensified exponentially by surviving the AIDS epidemic — while in the midst of it, colleagues, friends, boyfriends, clients, and acquaintances died left and right.

During my genealogy research, I obtained a copy of my mother's death certificate — which listed the name of the mortuary that handled her cremation. I called them on the off chance that — decades later — they could tell me where her ashes had been spread. My father had said he had no idea — just that it was "at sea."

They had no exact record, but said that at that time, given her place of death, they would have worked with a mortuary in Santa Barbara for this ritual. The mortuary in Santa Barbara had long ago expunged its records from the late 1970s, but the person I spoke with had been there long enough to know that at that time, unclaimed ashes were spread by boat a couple of times a week in — or more likely just outside — Santa Barbara Harbor.

Peter and I took a road trip north in the spring of 2023 — to visit with our old friend George in San Francisco and to explore the Paso Robles wine region a bit on the way south. We stopped off our first night in Santa Barbara, staying at the Castillo Inn, a block from the harbor.

Coffee in hand, early morning on the day after our arrival found me standing inside the harbor's seawall, looking out over the Pacific Ocean just beyond. For the first time, nearly forty-five years after her death, I was able to visit my mother's final resting place. I felt her there and then, finally — and was relieved that I could now pay my proper respects.

One expects later in life that one's parents will no longer be alive. One also begins to lose one's contemporaries, including siblings. But, honestly, it feels like a different lifetime today from the one in which all those essential souls who simply seemed as if they had always been, and always would be, were in fact there.

I'm not exactly sure what it means to still be here. Sharon and Nick in particular, but Michael, Siggy, Gregory, Dan and all the others who died from AIDS; Ray, Jerry, Suzanne, and all my other great pals from London; Tom, my SMC classmate, and Jimmy, my soulmate former student who both died much too young; Monique; and all the puppies who have been such healers, earth angels, and spirit guides throughout my life; not just Peter's and mine (Dugan, Jack, Bentley, and Fenway), but all their predecessors as well; Cookie and

Tom-Dog, Crotch and Sharon's pup, Fritz — all have moved on to more pure realms where we hope one day to join them.

The aggregate effect, internally, is one of having survived tremendous loss as part of the price I've paid to survive — and finding myself more alone in the present than I experience my contemporaries as being — who seem all to have more family, a larger circle of living friends, etc. I am of course at the same time enormously grateful that Margrethe, Leia, Carlos, George, close cousins, and a wide circle of friends and acquaintances from different parts of my life are still aboveground.

I take seriously today, having been told twice, that a part of my job is to also live for others who didn't get to, or who aren't blessed with the same freedoms. Michael in his dying days told me that, and the young North Africans whom Marti, Nick, and I met on the beach that last night before crossing the Mediterranean into Italy told us the same.

I feel the same duty to my siblings, Sharon and Ken, and to my other fellow trauma victims, especially those who did not survive to claim their lives and tell their own stories.

And it's a simple truth that I am immeasurably blessed to daily enjoy Peter's ultimately ineffable love and companionship, our mild Southern California climate, a quiet and comfortable life together, keeping our gardens, and visiting our favorite local wineries regularly with friends and neighbors.

Chapter Nineteen
Two Dreams – "The Jailer" and "Freedom-to-Roam"

I don't always remember my dreams, but two early-in-life ones have stayed with me and, looking back, seem somewhat prophetic.

I'll call the first one "The Jailer." Four of us lived in a fortresslike prison with high walls. The jailer/warden was a bug-eyed, seething, angry man — who bore a striking resemblance to my father. He seemed omnipresent, always on patrol, making sure that all was under (his) control and that no one escaped. His assistant — who had no real power of her own, save her wiles and a certain talent for subterfuge — was meek and subservient in the jailer's presence. Together with a smaller, younger child, I was imprisoned here; this was my home.

The assistant devised my escape; my books and my glasses would be the key to evading the jailer. The assistant would run interference. I had to do my part to make the plan work, and she would do hers. I wanted to take the smaller, younger child with me. The assistant said she could not guarantee that we both could escape. She seemed to accept that she herself could never escape.

I had been held physically captive by my father until I left home to go to SMC — and psychologically captive for many years after — primarily enslaved to my shame, until I was gradually able — using my education and my wits — to escape here as well, albeit not without significant wounds and residue.

I'll call the second dream "Freedom-To-Roam." In essence, I lived in a safe and comfortable home with good light and several rooms. My days were largely spent going peacefully from room to room, enjoying the changing of the light as the day progressed. There was no other person in this dream, though I was free to come and go and could certainly have invited companionship. There were no restrictions or impediments.

Dreams possess always their own logic and design. I have no idea why we were four and not five in the "The Jailer." "Freedom-To-Roam" seems like the antithesis of "The Jailer." I had indeed escaped and found safety, albeit alone, the only one who made it out. "The Jailer" quite aptly captures my childhood reality and seems to point to the life of the mind as my way out — rather than any physical escape, like climbing the walls. "Freedom-To-Roam," remarkably prescient, captures uncannily the essence of my life today — one I could not have foreseen or imagined years ago when I had the dream.

Despite its being an area of great interest — even fascination — to me, and one of significant study, and the subject of many client conversations over the years, I'm going to resist the temptation to launch into a thorough discussion of dreams and their interpretation here since I'm not sure that it would be relevant to this telling.

At the same time, in including the two described above, I am suggesting that the psyche has ways of knowing — and even predicting — that we generally do not recognize in this culture in the day-to-day (other cultures do a better job of this, in my opinion). Intuition is the essence of what I'm talking about here: a primary — perhaps *the* primary — form of intelligence that we humans are capable of.

I do seem to have been fated to be the designated survivor. And it has been my destiny to figure out what to do with that.

I enjoy social media — Facebook, TikTok, and Instagram especially. They allow staying in touch with family and friends, as well as former students and colleagues. They also allow me to visit other people's worlds — across generations and cultures and countries — whom I only know virtually — but enjoy knowing immensely, and would otherwise never know them at all.

I find it harmless and fun that birthday greetings flow between family, friends, and loved ones — and equally within the social-media online community — which comes to feel very real in its own way. I extend and receive hundreds every year — and can see and feel that others enjoy and appreciate them as I do.

Fathers and Sons

I can't conclude without a final reflection about my own father. I certainly had a biological father. He did provide materially for his family. We all were housed, clothed, and fed.

Aside from these aspects, he was AWOL. I didn't have a father — in fact, had a negative or minus father — an evil imposter who should never have been allowed access to me or any other child. It's a lack, a loss, a void, and an insult I shall never be able to correct.

Have I forgiven my father? I have not.

I recently witnessed the antithesis of my relationship with my father. Entirely without any trace of self-consciousness, nor an ounce of tension in any of their bodies, sat a radiant father with a son on either side, each with his head on one of their father's shoulders. The older boy was ten or eleven, the younger seven or eight; one was looking at his phone; the other held a book. They were sitting on a bench in the waiting room at the doctor's office as I was leaving. They seemed oblivious to their surroundings, utterly at peace with one another, the paternal version/vision of *Madonna and Child*. They oozed love, trust, affection, and safety. I melted internally at seeing them. Dad was clearly a deeply loving father; the boys were enveloped in and by his love.

Spain's Carlos Alcaraz, one of the era's most remarkable athletes, won the 2024 French Open Tennis Championship at age twenty-one. The winning point scored, he raced immediately to his box, where he fullheartedly embraced the many assembled members of his coaching team and extended family. Finally, saving them for last, he embraced his mother and father together — one tight and lingering embrace — before giving and receiving multiple kisses from each of them, his eyes moist with emotion.

Alcaraz frequently credits the love and support of his family — particularly his parents — as keys to his success.

Brittney Griner, in a 2024 interview with Joy Reid after her release from Russian prison, said of her ever-loving and supportive father, "That's my hero."

"No finer man," "So blessed," "If only I were half the man," "My best friend," "Such a lucky guy, I get to work with him" are amongst Father's Day accolades I see each year on social media that challenge — in some ways shock, humble, and remind — me of who my father was *not* to me, and the paternal absence I have experienced my entire life.

I admit to significant envy when I read these comments or witness a clearly loving and trusting father-son relationship as described above, whether in real life or in some form of media. It's not uncommon for me to choke up and be on the verge of tears when I witness this.

For me, such a bond bespeaks a distant and foreign planet — one I find exotic and hugely attractive, but punishingly illusive — one I cannot imagine ever occupying.

But, most of all, I revisit the constancy of grief and active mourning at what wasn't.

Chapter Twenty
Concluding Ramblings and Reflections – Surviving and Thriving

A great reservoir of sadness, to which I feel entirely entitled, dwells deeply in my soul. It's a part of me. I've tried in the past to ignore or escape it, but now I simply respect and accept it as a testimonial to the life I've lived. I'm aware that people can sometimes see and/or sense it; so be it.

There have long been moments — out of the blue — when I find myself feeling weepy. All the sadness and the loss and the grief comes to the surface, together with all the lives damaged and destroyed. So it all lives in my depths, and simply comes to visit whenever it pleases.

I retain an ever-present, spectral, illogical-to-the-adult, makes-perfect-sense-to-the-abandoned-little-boy-within waiting, still and always , for someone to finally find me, to come get me.

Trauma imprints and endures; it's indelible.

The weight of other people's projections (father, authority figure) — as therapist, teacher, boss/administrator — and the struggle to climb out from underneath them — and then to discover anew who it is and has been who dwells beneath — has been a welcome part of the work of my retirement and of writing this book.

Left with a certain stiffness/tensions that have long lived in my body (no music lives in me; I never could dance, as I mentioned earlier), social awkwardness (unless I have a role/purpose), a well-masked extreme introversion, a love of silence — all are constants in my moment.

Sartre is believed to have said, even very late in life, that he thought about sex constantly, every day. I can relate.

As mentioned above and at the beginning of the book, the frightened and abandoned little boy makes periodic appearances — often at the most inopportune times. He takes the wheel at will. When others experience him, I can see that they are dumbfounded. It's a bit as if a separate personality emerges from the depths — he totally takes control; he and I are one in those moments — and have always been.

Agatha Christie famously said, "I like living. I have sometimes been wildly, despairingly, acutely miserable, racked with sorrow; but through it all I still know quite certainly that just to be alive is a grand thing." I couldn't agree more.

I'm pretty confident that there is no "trauma survival guide" — and I certainly don't mean or intend to present one here. My story is going to be fundamentally different from others' stories, yet all these stories might overlap in some ways — intersect, illuminate, or reinforce one another.

If we're lucky enough to emerge more or less intact once we've thrown off the rubble of our trauma as best we are able, and have the good fortune to dwell in a safe place — physically, emotionally, spiritually — and look back, we can likely then begin to see how we survived, what price we paid to survive, and how our trauma continues to live inside and inform us even today.

I had no grand strategy for survival, and learned a lot about how I have managed to survive — and the enduring scars I retain — by writing this tale.

Trauma can drive us into ourselves, making us feel absolutely alone in the world, as if no one and no place is safe, and the idea of asking for help doesn't even occur to us. We all cope and react in different ways.

I believe in a universal life spirit that seeks the light, healing, wholeness — and to cast out the injury done to us. I know that sounds a bit grand and New Age, and even luxurious to some who were so beaten down, so pummeled by their trauma that they didn't have the residual strength to seek out this guiding light from within. And I acknowledge once again that trauma takes many lives and destroys many others. But for those of us fortunate enough to have the will and the luck and the energy to fight, we choose what "therapies" we can to assist us.

My therapies have been both conventional and unconventional, formal and informal, solitary and interactive. They have included LSD and THC, meditation, dogs, psychic readings and hypnotherapy, friendship, psychotherapy, silence, and solitude. Laughter, sex, and fun have played crucial roles as well. Each of us has her/his own therapies. They are lifesavers.

I have sought to surface and shatter my shame, and wrest myself free of its enslaving grip. Definite assists in my process include seeking out good people and staying away from the others; striving — looking forward, determined to move in that direction; establishing an internal sanctuary that nothing and no one can take from me; escaping in various forms, including within; making peace and finding richness in solitude and silence; giving back and trying to help others; working on not judging; being ever ready and willing to let go and move on.

Spirit was and is of major importance to me — embracing and deeply trusting some ineffable force greater than myself — and beneficent toward me — experienced in meditation, awe, and moments of grace, as white light, as a powerful peace and calm, as pure love.

Trusting my inner compass, my own north star — even when I could trust little else — has been essential. For years, I carried a small turtle totem in my pants pocket to remind myself, *Don't abandon yourself,* in whatever social or professional setting I happened to find myself. I often needed the reminder, as I, otherwise, very easily slipped into feelings of worthlessness and depression.

Curiosity, determination, stubborn independence; a certain fearlessness; humor, sarcasm, and irony help a lot — an appreciation of the divine farce.

When it comes to trusting others, I learned to trust but verify — over time, usually not right away.

I say, turn your trauma into a secret weapon; confuse people with how you got to be so resilient, tough, and perceptive. Flat-out refuse to capitulate. Shatter your shame, and take its power away. It doesn't deserve you!

Although not a practitioner of prayer in a religious sense, I love the acronym PUSH — Pray Until Something Happens — which can serve as a kind of mantra, ever hopeful that things can and will get better.

I learned to "sleep on it" when possible — no need to make snap decisions; this was a good counterbalance to my not-always-perfect, in-the-moment judgment.

I don't spend a lot of time or energy on the what-ifs. I try to learn and move on, focusing more on the present and the future than the past. I'm never 100-percent successful here, but it helps to have this as a goal.

The following require detachment: writing, photography, meditation, psychotherapy, me.

Peter and I live an inimitable depth of intimacy — meeting in mind, heart, and spirit — of which I am daily in a state of incredulity, awe, and deep gratitude — my crowning life-time achievement. Even so, it does battle with the parts of me that do not feel worthy or able. It, too, like "All the King's Men," in the Humpty-Dumpty children's rhyme, doesn't put ALL the pieces back together again, but I know that I have escaped to create, with a singularly remarkable soul, a reality I never witnessed — let alone experienced — as a child.

The Attic

We had contractors in to clean out and seal our attic, then double the insulation and add a whole-house fan to draw the tired, warmer air on summer nights up and out the attic vents, while ushering in the cooler evening air from outside, guaranteeing a comfortable night's sleep all through the hottest weather.

The process of writing this book has been somewhat analogous to our attic process. If, psychologically and spiritually, the attic is that shadowy, dark, and mysterious part of the house where we store away and forget about items from our past — and the memories attached to them — and an environment we rarely visit, such that who knows what creatures might also be living there, and we empty it out, seal it against unwelcome intruders, and fortify it with additional layers of protection, plus ensure our rest by constantly airing it out and keeping it fresh — then we've vanquished the detritus, the dark, mysterious sludge left behind by our trauma.

I have felt a great weight lift as I write this book. Secrets that hid in dark corners have now been exposed in the light of day. The shame that I have worn like a second skin all my life is being cast off; it no longer has the same power as before. I have reclaimed much of that which was stolen from me — and am more whole and alive inside than ever before. Confession truly IS good for the soul!

It has taken a while, granted, but when one perseveres, one can slay the monster and flourish — with just enough scar tissue to remind of the battles fought and the price paid and the wondrous accomplishment of being here to tell the tale.

There have been a series of thefts in high-income areas here in Southern California — homes targeted by sophisticated gangs from Eastern Europe and South America — break-ins in which high-value items that are easily sold are taken. Frequently, entry is gained by smashing a window or sliding-glass door when the homeowner is away. Police have a mixed record of recovering the items and catching the perpetrators.

Even when items are recovered and eventually returned, and the broken glass repaired, and new cameras and alarm systems installed — the homeowners don't feel entirely whole. They still feel violated, unsafe, and in need of being hyper-vigilant, where before they simply lived and enjoyed their lives; their trauma remains even after their items are returned and their homes repaired.

Trauma is a thief.

Alas, I've taken you on a journey of the inner and outer worlds my early life sent me off to explore — in hopes of finding lost parts of myself. Like my good ski instructor in the French Alps all those years ago, I'll leave you here now... in hopes that this tale might have had some value for you.

Thanks for reading and accompanying me.

Acknowledgments

When I finally had a VERY rough draft of the initial sections of this book in writing, I tracked down Janet Goldstein, who had been my editor with HarperCollins, and retained her to review and react to what I had written. I knew that her review would be brilliantly unsparing, which it was. I asked her to respond to my central question at the time: "Is there a 'there' there?"

Janet gave my initial effort a 5/10 and made several crucial critical suggestions on structure, focus, consistency of voice, etc. I thank her for that; it was exactly what I needed to move forward.

Lisa Umina, my publisher at Halo International, believed in me and the book from the start. I had the opportunity in my search for just the right publisher to interact with a number of possible alternatives. When Lisa and I signed off from our initial Zoom call, I was pretty sure that she was the one; by the end of our second, I was signing my contract with Halo.

Una Chester, my soulmate and editor, gets me and *Trauma Is a Thief* at a very deep level. She has been at once thorough and exact, while respectful and engaging of both me and the book. I am very grateful to Una and to Lisa for pairing us up as she did.

Lally Hoffmann and I have been very close friends for over half a century — but are both in denial about all that and are still kids at heart. She herself has traveled the world over and over in her work as a journalist, and for pleasure. Our paths have crossed many times in our travels. She has authored several books of her own. We have squabbled — like siblings — for decades, embraced therein by a great depth of love and respect. She has held my hand and cheered me on at every step of this process.

Peter, Peter, Peter: my rock. He has uncritically and unquestioningly supported this effort, giving me the space and benediction in our life together to allow *Trauma Is a Thief* to be born and come fully to life. My debt to him is immeasurable.

Let's Connect

Get to know Neal King, PhD

Wikipedia:
https://en.wikipedia.org/wiki/Neal_King
LinkedIn:
https://www.linkedin.com/in/neal-king-phd-6a623310/
Email:
NKingPhD@gmail.com

Printed in the USA
CPSIA information can be obtained
at www.ICGtesting.com
LVHW021343280924
792163LV00001B/4